CONSTRUCTING THE TEAM

by **Sir Michael Latham**

*Joint Review of Procurement and Contractual Arrangements
in the United Kingdom Construction Industry*

Final Report

July 1994

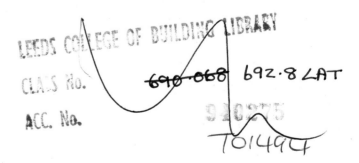

**Designed by
Design, Drawing and Print Services**
DEPARTMENT OF THE ENVIRONMENT

recycled paper

Contents

Last December, "Trust and Money" sought to identify the main issues of the Review, and invited comments and proposals. A very large number have been received. Public debate has been encouraging, wide ranging and serious.

This Final Report makes recommendations to tackle the problems revealed in the consultation process. The Review has been about helping clients to obtain the high quality projects to which they aspire. That requires better performance, but with fairness to all involved. Above all, it needs teamwork. Management jargon calls that "seeking win-win solutions". I prefer the immortal words of the Dodo in "Alice's Adventures in Wonderland", "Everybody has won and all must have prizes". The prize is enhanced performance in a healthier atmosphere. It will involve deeper satisfaction for clients. It will lead to a brighter image and better rewards for a great industry.

The issues of the Review provoke profound disagreement throughout the construction process. I could not deal with every problem raised with me, still less seek to solve them all. Some proposals which were made to me towards the end of the Review require further debate. I have tried to produce a balanced package which offers hope to all, reassurance to some, but despair to none.

This has not been a Government Review of the industry. It has been a Report commissioned jointly by the Government and the industry, with the invaluable participation of clients. It has been completed within a very tight pre-determined timetable to discharge extremely wide terms of reference. It is the personal Report of an independent, but friendly, observer. No blame attaches to anyone except myself for its contents. I have been immensely helped by many people, and especially by Deborah Bronnert of the Department of the Environment, to whom I am particularly grateful. But shortcomings or mistakes in this Report are my fault alone.

Some recommendations are radical. The participants in the construction process can react in three ways to them.

- They can refuse to have anything to do with the Report. That would be a pity. The problems would remain, but the goodwill to tackle them, which has been growing dramatically over the last twelve months, would be lost.

- They can pick out the sections which suit them and reject the rest. If everyone does that, nothing will happen.

- Or, hopefully, they can try to make the package work, through the implementation structures which the Report recommends. They can set about Constructing the Team.

The time to choose has arrived. The construction process cannot wait 30 years for another Banwell or 50 years for another Simon.

Michael Latham
July, 1994

1. Previous reports on the construction industry have either been implemented incompletely, or the problems have persisted. The opportunity which exists now must not be missed (Chapter 1, paragraph 1.10).

2. Implementation begins with clients. The Department of the Environment should be designated by Ministers as lead Department for implementing any recommendations of the Report which Ministers accept. Government should commit itself to being a best practice client. Private clients have a leading role and should come together in a Construction Clients' Forum. Clients, and especially Government, continue to have a role in promoting excellence in design (Chapter 1, paragraphs 1.17-1.19).

3. The state of the wider economy remains crucial to the industry. Many of the problems described in the Interim Report, and also addressed in this Final Report, are made more serious by economic difficulties. But others are inherent (Chapter 2).

4. Preparing the project and contract strategies and the brief requires patience and practical advice. The CIC should issue a guide to briefing for clients (Chapter 3, paragraph 3.13). The DOE should publish a simply worded Construction Strategy Code of Practice (Chapter 3, paragraphs 3.14 - 3.15) which should also deal with project management and tendering issues (Chapter 6).

5. The process plant industry should be consulted by the DOE, and be part of the Construction Clients' Forum (Chapter 3, paragraph 3.18).

6. A check list of design responsibilities should be prepared (Chapter 4, paragraph 4.6).

7. Use of Co-ordinated Project Information should be a contractual requirement (Chapter 4, paragraph 4.13).

8. Design responsibilities in building services engineering should be clearly defined (Chapter 4, paragraph 4.21).

9. Endlessly refining existing conditions of contract will not solve adversarial problems. A set of basic principles is required on which modern contracts can be based. A complete family of interlocking documents is also required. The New Engineering Contract (NEC) fulfils many of these principles and requirements, but changes to it are desirable and the matrix is not yet complete. If clients wish, it would also be possible to amend the Standard JCT and ICE Forms to take account of the principles (Chapter 5, paragraphs 5.18 - 5.21).

10. The structures of the JCT and the CCSJC need substantial change (Chapter 5, paragraphs 5.26 - 5.29 and Appendix IV).

11. Public and private sector clients should begin to use the NEC, and phase out "bespoke" documents (Chapter 5, paragraph 5.30). A target should be set of 1/3 of Government funded projects started over the next 4 years to use the NEC.

12. There should be a register of consultants kept by the DOE, for public sector work. Firms wishing to undertake public sector work should be on it (Chapter 6, paragraph 6.11).

13. A DOE-led task force should endorse one of the several quality and price assessment mechanisms already available for choosing consultants (Chapter 6, paragraph 6.11).

14. The role and duties of Project Managers need clearer definition. Government project sponsors should have sufficient expertise to fulfil their roles effectively (Chapter 6, paragraph 6.18).

15. A list of contractors and subcontractors seeking public sector work should be maintained by the DOE. It should develop into a quality register of approved firms (Chapter 6, paragraph 6.24). The proposed industry accreditation scheme for operatives should also be supported by the DOE (Chapter 7, paragraph 7.10).

16. Tender list arrangements should be rationalised, and clear guidance issued (Chapter 6, paragraph 6.32). Advice should also be issued on partnering arrangements (paragraph 6.47).

17. Tenders should be evaluated by clients on quality as well as price. The NJCC recommendations on periods allowed for tendering should be followed (Chapter 6, paragraph 6.39).

18. A joint Code of Practice for the Selection of Subcontractors should be drawn up which should include commitments to short tender lists, fair tendering procedures and teamwork on site (Chapter 6, paragraph 6.41).

19. Recent proposals relating to the work of the Construction Industry Training Board (CITB) need urgent examination (Chapter 7, paragraphs 7.16 - 7.18).

20. The industry should implement recommendations which it previously formulated to improve its public image. Equal opportunities in the industry also require urgent attention (Chapter 7, paragraph 7.25).

21. The CIC is best suited to co-ordinate implementation of already published recommendations on professional education (Chapter 7, paragraph 7.30).

22. Existing research initiatives should be co-ordinated and should involve clients. A new research and information initiative should be launched, funded by a levy on insurance premia (Chapter 7, paragraph 7.40).

23. More evidence is needed of the specific effects of BS 5750 within the construction process (Chapter 7, paragraph 7.46).

24. A productivity target of 30 per cent real cost reduction by the year 2000 should be launched (Chapter 7, paragraph 7.48).

25. A Construction Contracts Bill should be introduced to give statutory backing to the newly amended Standard Forms, including the NEC. Some specific unfair contract clauses should be outlawed (Chapter 8, paragraphs 8.9 - 8.11).

26. Adjudication should be the normal method of dispute resolution (Chapter 9, paragraph 9.14).

27. Mandatory trust funds for payment should be established for construction work governed by formal conditions of contract. The British Eagle judgement should be reversed (Chapter 10, paragraph 10.18).

28. The Construction Contracts Bill should implement the majority recommendations of the working party on construction liability law (Chapter 11, paragraph 11.15).

29. "BUILD" insurance should become compulsory for new commercial, industrial and retail building work, subject to a de minimis provision (Chapter 11, paragraph 11.24).

30. An Implementation Forum should monitor progress and should consider whether a new Development Agency should be created to drive productivity improvements and encourage teamwork. Priorities and timescales for action are suggested (Chapter 12).

1.1 The Joint Review of Procurement and Contractual Arrangements in the United Kingdom Construction Industry was announced to the House of Commons on 5th July 1993 (Hansard, Written Answers, Column 4). The Interim Report, entitled "Trust and Money", was published on 13th December 1993. The Under Secretary of State at the Department of the Environment (DOE), Mr Tony Baldry MP, also reported to the House of Commons on the same day in an answer to Mr Roger Sims MP (Hansard, Written Answers, Col. 454).

1.2 The funding parties to the Review have remained as stated in the Interim Report - the DOE, the Construction Industry Council (CIC), the Construction Industry Employers Council (CIEC), the National Specialist Contractors Council (NSCC) and the Specialist Engineering Contractors Group (SECG). Clients have continued to be closely involved in the Review, and are represented by the British Property Federation (BPF) and the Chartered Institute of Purchasing and Supply (CIPS). The terms of reference and details of the industry funding organisations are contained in Appendices I and II to this Report.

1.3 Throughout the Review, the four industry funding organisations and the two client groups have been represented by Assessors, and the Department of the Environment by the Director of the Construction Sponsorship Directorate. The Department has also provided the full time secretariat for the Review. Once again, it is my privilege to express the deepest possible thanks to those people who have given immense support and wise counsel to me. They have been:-

DOE	Mr Phillip Ward, Director, Construction Sponsorship Directorate
	Ms Deborah Bronnert, Assistant to the Reviewer
Clients	Mr Frank Griffiths, CIPS
	Mr William McKee, BPF
Consultants/Professionals	Mr Ian Dixon CBE, CIC
Main Contractors	Mr David Anderson, CIEC
Specialist Engineering Contractors	Mr Christopher Sneath, SECG
Specialist Trade Contractors	Mr Antony Carr, NSCC

All of them have devoted tremendous time and effort to this work, and I am most grateful to them. My gratitude also goes to the support groups which each of the organisations formed to guide their Assessors, and to the staff of those organisations on whom much additional work has fallen. I have had constant assistance and a speedy response to all the requests which I have made for information and guidance. Without such support, the work could not have been completed.

1.4 During the Review, the Assessors met 8 times as a group. They were never intended to be a decision making committee, still less a drafting body. Nor were they required to approve the Interim Report or this final document. They formed an expert sounding board and conduit of advice. But they became much more. A tremendous spirit of co-operation and mutual confidence soon emerged. We discussed highly contentious issues, which directly affected the livelihood and commercial prospects of their member organisations. Feelings on these issues run very deep, as my meetings and postbag have confirmed, and as I sought to indicate in the Interim Report. Over 100 Members of Parliament, including Cabinet and "Shadow" Cabinet Ministers, wrote to me expressing the concern of firms in their constituencies about aspects of the Review. It would not have been surprising if we had had angry meetings of the Assessors, perhaps even breakdowns in the discussions. Nothing could be further from the reality. The participants listened carefully to each other, weighed the contrasting arguments seriously, and frequently reconsidered their own views. It was said on several occasions that opinions had been changed by what had been heard. A person who had come into the meeting believing that his perspective was the only way to look at a problem came to realise that there were other genuine viewpoints.

1.5 That feeling has led some participants to urge that the understanding which has been achieved over the last twelve months should not be lost after the publication of this Report. I agree. The involvement of clients has been particularly significant. There have been many committees in the past which have brought together different parts of the construction industry. Some of them have reported directly to Ministers or been chaired by them. But the crucial change in recent years has been the grouping together of the many diverse interests into a small number of bodies, and the emergence of clients as major participants in the discussions. It would be unthinkable now for any new forum to be set up which did not include clients. Some of the organisations involved in the Review have suggested administrative structures for future work. I examine this later in the report and make recommendations accordingly.

1.6 As well as the Assessors, whom I have also met separately on frequent occasions, Ms Bronnert and I have had many meetings with groups, associations, companies, partnerships, academic institutions, Government Departments and individuals. So far as possible, we agreed to meet everyone who asked to see us, though for reasons of available time some people saw one of us but not both, and we had to bring the discussions to an effective end at Easter. A list of those meetings is set out in Appendix III. We are indebted to all who made themselves available in this way. Their contributions have been invaluable.

1.7 The Interim Report called for public debate and for proposals to assist the formulation of recommendations for the Final Report. A very large number have been received and all have been closely studied. A list of those papers has been compiled by the DOE for reference purposes. Many people have sent letters, which were also gratefully received and carefully considered.

1.8 The Interim Report sought:

1. To describe the background to the Review and its parameters.

2. To define the concerns of the differing parties to the construction process, some of which were mutually exclusive.

3. To pose questions about how performance could be improved and genuine grievances or problems addressed.

4. To reiterate and expand upon what has long been accepted as good practice in the industry but is often honoured more in the breach than in the observance.

1.9   The response to the Interim Report was generally positive. Most respondents felt that it had addressed the main issues. Some preferred to place emphasis upon certain findings rather than others. Some wanted a detailed look at new techniques and approaches which they believed would assist performance. Some totally new ideas have emerged since the Interim Report.

1.10   Many people have asked whether action would be taken to implement any proposals which the Final Report made. They pointed out that there had been widespread agreement on the Simon Report[1], the report by Sir Harold Emmerson[2] and the Banwell Report[3], but rather less action. Some of the recommendations of those reports were originally implemented. But other problems persisted, and do so to this day, even though the structure of the industry and the nature of many of its clients have changed dramatically. The initiative must be taken by Government, in conjunction with major clients and other leaders of the construction process. If this opportunity is not taken, it may not re-occur for many years, and a new report may be commissioned in the year 2024 to go over the same ground again!

Clients as the Driving Force

1.11   Implementation begins with clients. Clients are at the core of the process and their needs must be met by the industry. But clients are dispersed and vary greatly. Previously, Government acted as a monolithic client. That is not so now. Many in the industry are concerned that developments in the public sector have fragmented the client base even further. The National Joint Consultative Committee for Building (NJCC) stated: "Nowadays the NJCC has no means of ensuring that all housing associations, trust hospitals, grant maintained schools, private Government agencies, utilities companies, etc. are aware of the best current practice and changes in the construction industry..... We also notice individual Government Departments operating different procurement practices and that this has become more pronounced since the demise of the PSA. Unless an effective communication network is established, as the construction industry is called upon to play its part in the economic recovery, more and more cases of bad practice will come to light and the thrust of the Interim Report may be of no avail". (Letter from Mr Alan Turner, Chairman, NJCC, 31st March 1994.)

1.12   Concerns were also expressed in Scotland, both in discussions with the industry, and also in the report by the Royal Incorporation of Architects in Scotland (RIAS) entitled "Value or Cost" (published March 1994). That report commented "For many decades, construction in Scotland has been dominated by a small number of professionally organised client bodies [in the public sector]...In 1980 these appeared to account for almost 70% of all construction, directly or indirectly, within the country...From March 1989 it became clear that the life of such agencies was rapidly coming to an end... The consequence is that the principal commissioning clients in Scotland have been divested of their in-house professional skills".

---

[1]   *Report of the Central Council for Works and Buildings, chaired by Sir Ernest Simon: "The Placing and Management of Building Contracts", HMSO, 1944.*

[2]   *"Survey of Problems Before the Construction Industries", HMSO, 1962.*

[3]   *Report of the "Committee on the Placing and Management of Contracts for Building and Civil Engineering work", chaired by Sir Harold Banwell, HMSO, 1964.*

1.13 The policy of disbanding and privatising the Property Services Agency gave individual Government procurers more freedom to make their own arrangements. There is no need for, and I do not recommend, the reintroduction of a central procurement agency. The delegation of authority within the public sector to those best placed to assess local needs was a sensible and welcome move. But it is greatly in the interests of such clients to have the best advice and robust guidelines which will assist them to obtain value for money.

1.14 The role of Government as client, along with leading private sector clients and firms, is crucial if the objectives of this Review are to be met. Government Departments - and the wider public sector - should deliberately set out to use their spending power not only to obtain value for money for a particular project but also to assist the productivity and competitiveness of the construction industry, and thereby obtain better value for money generally in the longer term. The commitment by Government to this principle in the recent White Paper "Competitiveness - Helping Business to Win" (HMSO, May 1994) is a very welcome development. Government - in all its forms - will have a continuing relationship with the construction industry. Encouraging continuous improvements in productivity should be the driving force behind Government action as client, and the formulation of best practice should complement and contribute to this.

1.15 One Government Department should take the lead to ensure that best practice and the drive for improvement are implemented throughout the public sector as a whole. The Treasury Central Unit on Procurement (CUP) has done an excellent job in providing Guidance Notes. But its remit goes much wider than construction and its day to day contact with the industry is limited. Many of the recommendations in this report need central Government action. The DOE, and especially its Construction Sponsorship Directorate, is highly regarded in the construction industry for its practical approach to the industry's problems. It is one of the commissioning parties to this Review and has taken a major part in supporting the work of the Reviewer and the Assessors.

A Forum for Private Clients

1.16 Other participants - especially leading clients and firms - also have a substantial role to play in setting demanding standards and insisting upon improvements. However, there is currently no single focus for private sector clients. Such an organisation should be created to provide inter alia an influential voice, with responsibility for promoting forward thinking on key issues. It should involve the BPF, the CIPS, the European Construction Institute, the Construction Round Table and perhaps other interested bodies. It should not be a bureaucratic or costly organisation. It could initially be brought together by one of the existing bodies and have no additional staff of its own. Clients will have a vital role to play in ensuring the implementation of best practice, and they will also have most to gain from it. The creation of such a forum should be an immediate priority.

1.17 I therefore recommend that:

1. The Department of the Environment, and specifically its Construction Sponsorship Directorate, be designated by Ministers as the lead Department for implementing any recommendations of this Report addressed to Government which Ministers accept. The DOE should act closely with the Departments for Scotland, Wales and Northern Ireland, and also with individual procurer Departments.

2. Government should commit itself to being a best practice client. It should provide its staff with the training necessary to achieve this and establish benchmarking arrangements to provide pressure for continuing improvements in performance.

3. A Construction Clients' Forum should be created to represent private sector clients.

Patronage & Good Design

1.18 The Interim Report stressed the responsibility of all clients, but especially those in the public sector, to commission projects of which present and future generations can be proud. Performance, efficiency, fairness and team work are the principal concerns of this Review. But there is a significant role for clients in promoting good design. It does not necessarily involve high cost. Good design will provide value for money in terms of both total cost and cost-in-use. The energy and maintenance equations should be upper-most in the minds of the client and the designer, as well as the appearance of the facade and the effective use of space.

1.19 Government has an important role to play in this regard[4]. The Millennium Fund may provide some opportunities for landmark schemes. Patronage should emphasise not only the external appearance - important though that is - but also that the project should be effective for the purposes for which it is intended. A well designed building need not be to a high level of specification. Evidence to the Review has suggested that some UK buildings are over specified and thus unnecessarily costly[5]. A well designed project will impact upon the satisfaction, comfort and well being of its occupants, and, if it is a commercial building, upon their productivity and performance. Government as patron is not an obsolete role. Quality should be the overriding consideration. The appointment of a special adviser on urban design to the Secretary of State for the Environment is a welcome recognition of the DOE's leading role in encouraging excellence. The Department of National Heritage also takes a constructive interest in the quality of design and the Secretary of State for National Heritage has a special adviser on architecture.

---

[4] *Several publications have criticised the Government's performance in this area. See the Royal Fine Art Commission's "Medicis and the Millennium? - Government Patronage and Architecture" by Judy Hillman, HMSO, 1992 and "Architecture and executive agencies", the Architecture Unit of the Arts Council, 1993.*

[5] *This concern is expressed in the final reports of the CIPS, "Productivity and Costs", of the SECG, "A Framework for the Future" and of the CIEC, all April 1994. See also Chapter 7 of this Report and the recent (May 1994) document from the British Council for Offices entitled "Specification for Urban Offices". The BCO document sets out a proposed draft specification, which was out for consultation as this Report went to press.*

2.1   There is no shortage of statistics about the construction industry. It contains 200,000 contracting firms, of which 95,000 are private individuals or one person firms. Only 12,000 contracting firms employ more than 7 people. (Source: DOE, 1992. All figures are approximate.) About 45% of registered architects are sole principals, or employ five qualified staff or less (source: RIBA, 1993). The value of output in the whole industry in 1993 was £46.3 billion, which represented about 8% of Gross Domestic Product (source: DOE). Large construction firms (employing 80 people or more) carried out over 40% of the workload by value in 1992. The industry is vital to the economy. Most people in the contracting sector work alone, or in small firms, but a limited number of large firms undertake a substantial proportion of the work.

2.2   The public sector is a less dominant client than it used to be. Some previously extensive programmes such as local authority housebuilding have been greatly reduced. Other work is now partly funded by private investment, or has been totally privatised. Privatisation has also involved the transfer of many professional services to the private sector which were previously carried out "in house" by Government Departments or local authorities. New procurers have appeared such as Executive Agencies, National Health Service Trusts or educational bodies such as Colleges of Further Education. Government has ceased to be a single procurer. The untying of Departments from the Property Services Agency has resulted in the emergence of a wide range of procurement techniques. There are now about 90 separate Government procurement bodies.

2.3   Client profiles in civil engineering have also been changing. According to a survey carried out by the Federation of Civil Engineering Contractors (FCEC), 60% of the workload of its member firms in 1991/1992 was carried out for public sector clients, and the remaining 40% for private sector clients, compared with only 10% in the late 1970s. A breakdown is given in box 1 overleaf.

BOX 1

PUBLIC SECTOR

- 23% for the Department of Transport, Scottish Office and Welsh Office on motorways and trunk roads;
- 11% for local councils on local roads;
- about 5% for the Ministry of Defence;
- 4/5% for British Rail and London Underground, and Public Sector Light Railways;
- about 3% at ports and airports, and waterways still in the public sector;
- over 2% for Scottish Local Authorities (Water and Sewerage);
- about 3% for Nuclear Electric;
- about 4% for British Coal;
- and about 2% for flood defence works.

PRIVATE SECTOR

- nearly 14% for the water industry in England and Wales;
- over 7% in private sector transport infrastructure;
- nearly 6% for energy industries;
- and nearly 7% site preparation connected with private building projects.

Box 1   *"Survey of Civil Engineering Workload Mix 1991/92", FCEC 1992*

2.4 The industry remains dependent upon wider economic stability. I wrote in the Interim Report that it was no part of my duty to advise upon Government economic policy generally. Some respondents to the enquiry have criticised that, but it must remain the case. The Government is responsible to Parliament, and through it to the electorate, for the conduct of the economy. I have not been asked to make recommendations about it.

2.5 However, some general observations are necessary because economic factors lie behind many of the issues addressed by the Review.

1. If the flow of work to the industry is less than the capacity available, a number of consequences follow:-

   a. firms will reduce their staff, or may close altogether;

   b. fee bids by consultants will become extremely keen, and may not allow the successful bidder to make any profit out of the commission;

   c. tender prices submitted by contractors will be uneconomically low, with adverse effects on all participants in the construction process;

   d. training and education will suffer;

   e. little money will be available for research and development or for enhancing the public image of the industry.

The CIEC comments in its final report to the Review (April 1994) that, since 1989, almost half a million jobs have been lost in the industry, training has fallen by over 50% and over 35,000 small businesses and companies have become insolvent.

2. Government directly affects construction workload by:-

    a. financing of public projects. This is particularly important in civil engineering;

    b. influencing the general level of demand in the economy. That determines the purchasing power and willingness of clients to proceed with construction investment.

2.6   The recession of recent years has hit the construction industry very hard, though hopefully some improvement in trading conditions is now beginning. It affected the construction industry more deeply than other industries. By 1993, construction output was still some 39% below its 1990 peak, whereas for manufacturing the dip was 3% and for services any lost growth has now been regained (source: CSO, 1994). Many of the industry's problems have been worsened by economic difficulties, though some were inherent and some exist in other countries as well. Government remains vital to construction. If the economy is weak, the industry will suffer, and its participants will try to alleviate that suffering at the expense of others (including clients). It is not easy to create teamwork in construction when everyone is struggling to avoid losses. If the economy is going wrong, little will go right in the construction industry.

2.7   Many of the core decisions are in the hands of Government. The industry has complained for many years that it should not be used as an economic regulator. It has almost ceased to believe that Government can, or ever will, resist the temptation to affect its livelihood through public expenditure restrictions or fiscal/monetary policies. It has taken steps to fill the gaps by turning to private financing, or joint activities with public clients, or overseas work. But the level of domestic construction work load is ultimately determined by Government economic policy. The industry can redistribute the work available amongst its participants through normal competitive forces. It can seek to bolster the purchasing power of clients through joint funding techniques. But it cannot create its core activities out of nothing. If there is more work around, there may be more money for efficient firms. If there is more money, there may be more trust. This is not a "begging bowl" approach, or a lack of a "can/do" attitude. It is a simple statement of commercial reality. It pervades virtually every decision taken every day by every participant in the construction process.

3.1 The recommendations in this Report are intended to benefit clients by improving the industry's performance and teamwork and thereby achieve better value for money. The Interim Report identified clients as the core of the construction process. Clients vary. Some are well informed, know what they want and take decisive steps to achieve it. Some, such as Stanhope, British Airports Authority plc and large retail chains, have emerged as leaders of the construction process, introducing new methods and techniques of procurement and site performance. Some are knowledgeable but not necessarily modern in their approach. Others are feeling their way under new administrative arrangements, including some Government Departments and Agencies. Some know nothing about the construction industry. They need extensive help and guidance to formulate their wishes and then match them to the available budget.

3.2 Clients will commission projects which contribute to their wider objectives. Their wishes will also normally include the following:-

1. value for money;

2. pleasing to look at;

3. free from defects on completion;

4. delivered on time;

5. fit for the purpose;

6. supported by worthwhile guarantees;

7. reasonable running costs;

8. satisfactory durability.

Clients do not always get what they asked for. Some are very critical, as table 1, presented to a construction industry conference on 15th December 1993 by a major procurer in the private sector, made clear.

Industry Performance Compared to Car Industry

Wants	Modern Motor Car	Modern Buildings		
		Domestic	Commercial	Industrial
Value-for-money	●●●●	●●●●●	●●●	●●●●
Pleasing to look at	●●●●	●●●●	●●●	●●●
(largely) Free from faults	●●●●●	●●●	●	●●
Timely Delivery	●●●●	●●●●	●●●●	●●●●
Fit-for-purpose	●●●●●	●●●●	●●	●●●
Guarantee	●●●●●	●●●●	●	●
Reasonable running costs	●●●●	●●●●	●●	●●●
Durability	●●●●	●●●	●●	●●
Customer delight	●●●●●	●●●	●●	●●

Source: Presentation by Dr Bernard Rimmer, Slough Estates plc, to a conference organised by "Contract Journal" & CASEC, the Barbican, London, 15th December 1993.

3.3 Such criticisms may be challenged by the industry as exaggerated, or unfair. But if clients express them, the industry has a problem. They must not be ignored. Some clients, including Slough Estates, have taken steps to enhance the level of consumer satisfaction for themselves and their tenants/occupiers.

3.4 A common cause of complaint by the industry is that the client does not know its own mind. An inadequate brief is presented to the consultant and/or the contractor. The client subsequently requires detailed changes in the work, with serious implications for cost and programme. Formulation of a project strategy by the client is the first building block to a successful and cost effective scheme. The route that should be followed is set out in box 2 below.

BOX 2

- The client perceives a need for new construction or refurbishment.

- An internal assessment is made which considers benefits, risks and financial constraints. It lists options for carrying out the project.

- Those options are put in order of benefits and feasibility. This may require external advice. The CUP (then the Public Competition and Purchasing Unit) suggested in Guidance Note 33 "Project Sponsorship" that a Professional Adviser be retained, whose work might largely finish with the appointment of a Project Manager.

- At that point, the client takes a decision in principle as to whether the project is necessary or feasible at all.

Box 2: Project Strategy

3.5 Some believe that this project strategy stage should involve likely participants in the project itself, and in particular the leader of the consultant team. For example, the DOE's manual of Guidance for Departments "Contracting for Works Services", volume III, "Responsibilities of Professional Consultants", begins its chapter on pre-design with "The Project Manager's contract with the client will have required the PM to install procedures to be followed by support consultants and control staff concerned with the project". It makes clear that a Project Manager is directly involved in the definition of need, while also stressing that the consultant may not necessarily become the PM for any further stages.

3.6 Many clients will undertake their own project strategy/need definition in-house. Those who are unable to do so are well advised to retain some external expert, but not initially in the title of **Project Manager**. Such a consultant is there to help the client decide if the project is necessary. If the "Professional Adviser" (as in CUP Guidance Note 33 terminology) has been retained in the expectation of becoming lead consultant for the project, it will place a substantial strain upon that individual to advise the client that the project is not needed at all or, if it is, that it could be a very small scheme which required no further consultant advice. Any client who wants external advice over project strategy and need definition should only retain an adviser on the express understanding that the role will terminate once the decision has been formulated on whether or not to proceed[6].

---

[6] *In its final report, the CIC draws attention to the consultancy service of the Royal Incorporation of Architects in Scotland, which seeks to give clients practical and objective advice about their procurement strategies before any decisions have been made.*

3.7 Once a client is satisfied about real need and feasibility within overall budgetary constraints, the instinctive reaction is to retain a consultant to design the project - the "ring up an architect/engineer" syndrome. That takes a crucial step too quickly, and closes off potential procurement options. The next step should be the use of internal risk assessment to devise a contract strategy. The client should decide how much risk to accept. No construction project is risk free. Risk can be managed, minimised, shared, transferred or accepted. It cannot be ignored. The client who wishes to accept little or no risk should take different routes for procuring advice from the client who places importance on detailed, hands-on control.

3.8 The basic decision on the procurement route should precede the preparation of the outline (project) brief, since it necessarily affects who shall assist with the design brief as well. That choice of route must be determined by the nature of the project and the clients' wishes over acceptance of risk. Such decisions are difficult. Inexperienced clients need advice. There are a number of publications which can assist.

3.9 Tables 2 and 3 summarise the distribution of risk under the respective Standard Forms of Contract, and how the client may broadly assess it in advance.

TABLE 2: CONTRACT OPTIONS

Contract options

RISK

Client   *Contractor*

MANAGEMENT		
PRIME COST	% Fee	
	Fixed fee	
APPROX QUANTS	Remeasured	
LUMP SUM	Fluctuations	
	Fixed price	
DESIGN AND BUILD		
PACKAGE DEAL		

Fundamental risks

Pure and particular risks

Speculative risks

1. Fundamental risks: War damage, nuclear pollution, supersonic bangs

2. Pure risks: Fire damage, storm

3. Particular risks: Collapse, subsidence, vibration, removal of support

4. Speculative risks: Ground conditions, inflation, weather, shortages and taxes

Source: figure 4, page 82 of "The Shorter Forms of Building Contract", 3rd edition by Hugh Clamp published by Blackwell Scientific Publications, 1993.

TABLE 3: SUMMARY OF ADVANTAGES AND DISADVANTAGES OF CONTRACT STRATEGIES

Project Objectives		Appropriateness of Contract Strategy in Meeting Project Objectives				
Parameter	Objectives	Traditional	Construction Management	Management Contracting	Design & Manage	Design & Build
Timing	Early Completion	□	■	■	■	■
Cost	Price certainty before construction start	■	□	□	□	■
Quality	Prestige level in design and construction	■	■	■	■	□
Variations	Avoid prohibitive costs of change	■	■	■	■	■
Complexity	Technically advanced or highly complex building	□	■	■	□	□
Responsibility	Single contractual link for project execution	□	□	□	□	■
Professional Responsibility	Need for design team to report to sponsor	■	■	■	■	□
Risk Avoidance	Desire to transfer complete risk	□	□	□	□	■
Damage Recovery	Ability to recover costs direct from the contractor	■	□	■	■	■
Buildability	Contractor input to economic construction to benefit the department	□	■	■	■	□

■ - appropriate   □ - not appropriate

[CUP Note: This table is for guidance only. Generally the appropriateness of the contract is not as clear cut as indicated. The project manager must advise the project sponsor on this.]

Source: CUP Guidance Note 36 "Contract Strategy Selection for Major Projects", June 1992.

3.10   Guidance on risk assessment for clients is crucial. It determines contract strategy. A range of procurement and contractual routes is emerging to meet clients' wishes. They are set out in box 3 below.

BOX 3

STANDARD CONSTRUCTION

The client and its advisers decide that the end product can be achieved through a pre-determined construction route, probably involving a limited range of standardised processes and components. This is best served by a design and build contract, with single point responsibility and the transfer of risk by the client. The contractor will be responsible for delivering the entire package. The amount of design provided by the client to the contractor will vary. It may involve the novation of some consultants to the contractor. The client retains an employer's agent to liaise with the contractor.

"TRADITIONAL" CONSTRUCTION

These projects involve well used and normal techniques of design and construction, but reflect specific wishes of the client. Most work is currently done on this basis, involving Standard Forms such as JCT 80 or ICE 5th/6th. This is the route with which the industry is most familiar. But it is also where many of the problems emerge through lack of co-ordination between design and construction. Problems can however be minimized or avoided by effective pre-planning of the design process, and efficient administration of the project by the client's representative, whatever title or designation that representative is given. An alternative is to use a combination of routes through design and manage approaches. The consultants, working for a lead manager, design and cost the scheme within their normal professional roles. They can then be paid their fees and discharged, after certifying that their responsibilities for the design are complete. The implementation of the design is then passed to a management contractor who is paid a fee to mobilise a series of works contractors to build the project. The client retains an employer's agent to liaise with the contractor.

INNOVATIVE CONSTRUCTION

The client commissions a project which involves a high degree of innovation, and many new design details. The client wants hands-on involvement and seeks strong management to produce the intended result. The best route here is construction management. It is a demanding procurement system, requiring firm leadership and team work throughout. There is no intrinsic reason why it should be limited to large or exceptionally prestigious schemes. It is also favoured by specialist/trade contractors because of its separate trade contract system. Some main contractors now offer this service, as do specialist construction management companies.

BOX 3   *Main Procurement and Contractual Routes*

3.11 Once a prospective client has decided that a project should proceed in principle, and roughly how much risk and direct involvement to accept, the project and design briefs can be prepared. The client who knows exactly what is required can instruct the intended provider. That may involve either appointing a Project Manager, or a client's representative to liaise with the designers, or a lead designer, or a contractor for direct design and build procurement. Even the best clients are likely to benefit from some advice on alternative methods of achieving their aim, which may produce better value for money. Most clients require detailed advice[7]. Getting the design brief right is crucial to the effective delivery of the project. The lead adviser must be given time to assist the client with the preparation of that brief. This should be an iterative process. Stages A & B of the RIBA "Plan of Work" are described as "Inception" and "Feasibility". The client will already have taken some basic procurement decisions on these matters. But whether or not the scheme is designer-led, the client must allow time and space for its wishes as expressed in the project brief to be further tested for the purpose of the design brief against questions of feasibility. Time may also be needed for other advisers - including the essential mechanical and engineering design/construction input - to be called in at these early stages. Commercial pressures from the client may require the detailed designs to be prepared sequentially. But clients will benefit by allowing enough time for a good brief to be devised in order to avoid subsequent delays and cost overruns in the project.

3.12 There should be a distinction between the project brief - the basic objectives of the client - and the design brief which comprises the client's specific requirements. The CIC, in its final report, recommends a comprehensive standard questionnaire and check list to assist the client in the briefing process. But the Royal Institute of British Architects (RIBA) believes that a "check list of standard subjects will necessarily be too general and rudimentary to be of much relevance" (RIBA evidence, April 1994). The CIEC's final report also favours an "authoritative guide" for clients to help "produce a comprehensive, agreed design brief", and points out that a good deal of work has already been done in this regard by various organisations.

---

[7] *The Association of Consultant Architects (ACA), in stressing the need for many clients to receive help with their brief, divides the design process into three stages:-*

(1) *The development of a statement of the client's intent. The design lead consultant should rigorously analyze any document received from the client, and the assumptions contained in it.*

(2) *The designer responds with concept sketches, and innovation in design usually occurs at this stage.*

(3) *The development of the sketches, with the design team and with the professional construction team. Design for procurement is likely to begin here. (ACA evidence, March 1994.)*

Recommendation 2: Guide for Clients on Briefing

3.13   Such a guide to briefing would be helpful to clients. I recommend that the CIC, in conjunction with clients, should prepare such a check list. It should also be part of the contractual process that the client should approve the design brief by "signing it off".

Recommendation 3: Code of Practice

3.14   DOE should co-ordinate and publish a Construction Strategy Code of Practice (CSCP) to inform and advise clients. It should be in simple terms and easy to read. It should be circulated to all Government Departments and Agencies, and also to other public sector institutions such as local Government, hospital trusts and health authorities and self governing educational institutions. It should be suitable for distribution to bodies representing private sector clients (including organisations such as Chambers of Commerce) and should be vigorously promoted by the DOE and by client organisations. It should be applicable throughout the United Kingdom, with appropriate sections on Wales, Scotland and Northern Ireland.

Recommendations 4 (1) to 4 (8)

3.15   The guidance in the CSCP should be designed to assist clients to meet their objectives and to obtain value for money. The Code should also be designed to harness clients' purchasing power to improve the long term performance of the industry. It should stress[8]:-

1. The wishes of clients must be paramount for all construction participants, subject to planning and development control and the wider public interest.

2. Clients should formulate a project strategy, which must involve need assessment and consideration of resources available.

3. Any external expertise retained to help with such a preliminary feasibility study should be for that purpose alone, and then discharged.

4. If a decision is made in principle to go ahead, the client should decide upon a contract strategy. It will be influenced by the amount of risk desired to be accepted, since that must directly affect the procurement route which is suitable for the project.

5. The advisers retained after that stage will be those who are most appropriate for that procurement route.

6. Those advisers will be crucial in assisting the client with the brief. This should be an iterative process, and adequate time must be allowed. If the brief is inadequate, the project will face avoidable difficulties throughout its life.

7. Clients should be strongly advised to consider cost-in-use and the impact which the scheme will have on the productivity of their business.

8. The client should "sign off" approval of the brief.

---

[8] *Further recommendations for the CSCP are contained in Chapter 6.*

3.16 Large engineering projects in the process plant sector of construction require detailed design and planning before commitment. The contract strategy may involve performance specifications being issued by the client, evidence being required that contractors have successful experience of a similar project, and possibly a condition that the successful tenderer should operate the plant or product after completion. The managing contractor is likely to offer full Engineer-Procure-Construct (EPC) capabilities. The European Construction Institute, which gave evidence to the Review, both directly and through the CIPS, stressed:-

1. Economies at the design phase will be self-defeating. Designers should not be selected on the basis of price. 10-15% of the total cost of a high technology project should be spent in this phase.

2. Where prototype equipment is involved, it must be identified in the initial stage of the project. Detailed programmes for research, design, testing and manufacture must be produced and monitored by the client. This should all be available before work starts on site.

3. Failure of material flow to the site or design changes can lead to unmanageable situations. Designs should be frozen and fully developed before the manufacture and site construction begins.

4. A "key date" procedure for discussing cash flow and resources at a very high level is vital every three months or so, as well as normal project progress meetings. Payments should be made properly and on time, provided that milestones have been achieved. The Project Manager should also be aware of whether the main contractor is paying the subcontractors on time, so as to prevent problems on site.[9]

3.17 Effective partnering between client and contractor with teamwork and a "win-win" approach helped to bring the Sizewell nuclear power station to completion on time and within budget[10]. But that client believes that there is still scope for further improvements in productivity and cost reduction, especially if design and construction teams could be kept together.[11]

---

[9] See also "Construction Contract Arrangements in EU Countries", European Construction Institute 1993, which gives valuable case studies of successful large projects.

[10] Speech to the CIPS conference on 30 March 1994 by Mr Brian George, Executive Director, Engineering, Nuclear Electric plc.

[11] An interesting study of the UK oil and gas industry was undertaken in 1993 entitled "CRINE" (Cost Reduction Initiative for the New Era). It is concerned with improving performance in oil and gas exploration and production. It makes similar recommendations to those in this Report, such as using standard equipment and simplifying and clarifying contract language and eliminating adversarial clauses. It is claimed in the report that the recommendations will lead to "at least a 30% reduction in capital costs within 2-3 years and to lower operating costs".

3.18   The process plant industry clients and contractors have much to contribute to further work following this Review. I recommend elsewhere that the European Construction Institute, as part of a Construction Clients' Forum, should be involved in the implementation strategy of this Report. The Institute feels that the DOE has not treated process plant clients as part of construction for consultation purposes. While industrial giants such as the chemical industry, Nuclear Electric or National Power will have much to discuss with the Department of Trade and Industry, it is important that their perspectives on construction should be heard by the DOE, and they should be consulted accordingly.

4.1 Effective management of the design process is crucial for the success of the project. It should involve:

1. A lead manager.

2. The co-ordination of the consultants, including an interlocking matrix of their appointment documents which should also have a clear relationship with the construction contract.

3. A detailed check list of the design requirements in the appointment documents of consultants. This should also be set out in the main contract documentation.

4. Ensuring the client fully understands the design proposals.

5. Particular care over the integration of building services design, and the avoidance of "fuzzy edges" between consultants and specialist engineering contractors.

6. The use of Co-ordinated Project Information.

7. Signing off of the various stages of design when they have been achieved, but with sufficient flexibility to accommodate the commercial wishes of clients.

4.2 The position of the lead manager or Project Manager is discussed in Chapter 6. The chosen procurement route will affect the design strategy and the employment of consultants. But it does not alter the need for all design to be co-ordinated.

Integrated Design

4.3 There must be integration of the work of designers and specialists. A design team for building work may include an architect, structural engineer, electrical services engineer, heating and ventilating services engineer, public health engineering consultant, landscape architect and interior designer. Some or all may have further specialists working either with them or for them. Installers - contractors, subcontractors and sub subcontractors - are also likely to have design responsibilities.

4.4   A graphic description of the complexity of the design process, and its potential for lack of co-ordination, was submitted to the Review by Mr James Nisbet, a senior chartered quantity surveyor[12] and former President of the Quantity Surveyors' Division of the Royal Institution of Chartered Surveyors (RICS).

"Architects are expected to produce working drawings and the builder is expected to carry out works in accordance with such drawings.   The structural engineer relies upon the manufacturers to design the connections for a steel frame.   The services engineer expects a subcontractor, appointed after the builder, to prepare all installation (i.e. working) drawings.   Design co-ordination before construction starts is therefore impossible and ad hoc alterations on site are inevitable.   Further, the tender and contract procedures adopted by architects and service engineers are at variance one with the other and this leads to difficulties and animosity in the management of cost and the administration of the contract conditions.   Architects' designs are usually the subject of Bills of Quantities but services engineers resolutely require tenders to be based on drawings and specifications.   The common range of conditions of contract place responsibility for the cost of a project solely upon one person, usually an architect or engineer.   The procedures adopted by the services engineer effectively prevent the architect or engineer from exercising control over the cost of the services element of a project.   Urgent attention should therefore be given to the elimination of this muddle."

4.5   A detailed check list of the design process is required so that responsibilities can be clearly allocated amongst the designers[13].   The British Property Federation's Manual contains a detailed check list in its Appendix I, and a draft Building Services Research and Information Association (BSRIA) report[14] does the same in more detail for building services engineers.   The client should ensure that all consultants are appointed under mutually interlocking contracts which specifically define their duties and responsibilities and set timescales for their implementation.   The lead manager and/or design leader should then take responsibility for co-ordinating the work of all the consultants[15].   This also needs to be set out in the main contract documentation.   It is vital that the contractor knows who is responsible for which elements of the design and when they will be available.

---

[12]   *Evidence by Mr James Nisbet, March 1994.   Mr Nisbet also kindly supplied a copy of his book "Fair and Reasonable - Building Contracts from 1550", Stoke Publications 1993.   Conditions of contract in the Middle Ages were clearly onerous.   A contract in York in 1335 required the carpenter to complete work within three months on pain of excommunication.   A mason failing to complete a contract for the Duke of York in 1434 was threatened with prison and confiscation of property and goods! (Nisbet, op. cit, page 12)*

[13]   *There is a schedule of services to be provided by the architect in SFA/92 ("Standard Form of Agreement for the Appointment of an Architect").   But it clearly does not satisfy some clients. "The standard document is very poor in this connection, particularly the RIBA Agreement SFA/ 92" (BPF final report to the Review, page 4).*

[14]   *"The Allocation of Design Responsibilities for Building Engineering Services - a code of conduct to avoid conflict", compiled by C J Parsloe, unpublished draft of May 1994.   Publication of the report was scheduled for July 1994 as this Report was going to the printers.*

[15]   *In some projects the client's representative, the lead manager and the design leader may be the same person.*

Recommendation 6: Check-List for Designers

4.6 The formulation of a full check list, or the adoption of existing ones such as those of the BPF or BSRIA, should be an urgent task of the reconstituted Joint Contracts Tribunal as part of their new duties as recommended in Chapter 5. As each stage of design is completed, the consultant should sign it off accordingly.

The Client - Understanding the Design

4.7 The design leader must ensure that the client fully understands the design proposals, and agrees that they meet its objectives. It is rarely satisfactory for clients to be shown conceptual drawings, still less outline plans of rooms. The design team must offer the client a vision of the project in a form which it can understand and change in time.

4.8 Models are useful, but an exciting new development is "Knowledge Based Engineering" (KBE). This system has been developed in manufacturing industry, both for aeroplanes and cars. It enables product managers and designers to see new ideas either through advanced computer aided design or "Virtual Reality". All aspects of the design, manufacture, assembly and use of the product can then be presented in one entity. Research carried out by the University of Reading and the British Airports Authority is showing that it is possible to use KBE in the design of individual construction projects. This development could have a massive effect in placing real choices before clients, and promoting better construction performance. If clients can clearly understand the likely outcome of projects at design stage, their wishes can be better met. Some industry experts believe that KBE is the technology of the 21st century, and that the software needed will be too complex and expensive for all but the most prestigious projects commissioned by the wealthiest clients. I suspect that the information technology revolution will produce speedier solutions than that, and will be client driven. Paying a higher fee to the designers for such information will be repaid many times over if it ensures a well planned project which meets the client's aspirations. The establishment of common standards for the exchange of electronic data would be highly desirable and further consideration should be given to this issue.

Co-ordinated Project Information

4.9 The Co-ordinated Project Information (CPI) initiative arose from work by the Building Research Establishment (BRE) in the 1970s. That revealed serious deficiencies in preparing the information necessary for the builder. Following further work within the industry, the Co-ordinating Committee for Project Information published its Codes of Procedure for Production Drawings, Project Specification and a Common Arrangement of Work Sections for Building Work in 1987. These Codes also co-ordinated with the newly published Standard Method of Measurement (SMM) 7. The initiative was supported by DOE Ministers. CPI has been adopted in the National Building Specification and in other influential documents. But its use is still limited, and the Building Project Information Committee (BPIC) is seeking to persuade more Schools of Architecture and Design to include CPI within their curricula. BPIC is also participating in the development of an international classification system for construction information. (Source: BPIC[16] evidence, February 1994.)

---

[16] *BPIC comprises representatives from the Building Employers Confederation (BEC), the RIBA, the RICS and the Chartered Institute of Building Services Engineers (CIBSE).*

4.10   To achieve co-ordination in the documents available to the constructors on site seems basic common sense.   As one client commented "If Knowledge Based Engineering is tomorrow's technology for construction, CPI ought to be yesterday's.   Surely we can harmonise the basic works information?"   The CIEC's final report also recommends the use (with some modifications) of CPI in civil engineering.

4.11   Some may wonder whether full design preparation of the project in this way is practical and really reflects clients' wishes and work patterns.   The reality of many commercial schemes is that the client dictates the pace of design by responding to external pressures from funders, potential supply/demands of tenants or other considerations.   If the client wishes work to start on site before the scheme is fully designed, and requires the drawings to be prepared sequentially, the system must adapt to that.   It is best practice if all projects are fully planned, as has been recommended by previous reports such as Banwell.   That remains the ideal.   But, as the ACA comments in its evidence, "This assumes perfection and no changes of circumstance in time, demand or finance.   If the client is the core of the need for an industry's response, should the processes of the industry <u>not</u> allow these changes to be made?   The answer must be yes, and without recrimination."   (ACA evidence, March 1994.)

4.12   I agree.   The system must be robust enough to meet the wishes of clients, not vice versa.   But:-

1.   The client whose commercial requirements demand an early start on site and sequential design during the course of the work should choose a procurement route which will accommodate those wishes in a flexible manner and which avoids adversarial attitudes.   Construction management or management contracting will be most appropriate.   A lump sum contract such as JCT 80 or a design and build route would be a recipe for disaster[17] if the work is intended to progress on site while design is still proceeding.

2.   It is still both practicable and desirable to use CPI in such circumstances.   The Codes and SMM 7 recognise that certain elements of the work may not have been fully designed when the contractor was preparing the tender.   SMM 7 therefore provides for the use of provisional sums for both defined and undefined work.   Use of CPI is possible regardless of when the information is produced, pre or post tender, and irrespective of the contract documentation used.

---

[17]   *An example which illustrates the potential pitfalls was the New Glasshouse at the Efford Experimental Horticultural Centre, Hampshire.   The appraisal first estimate in August 1989 was £0.25 million.   The contract price in December 1989 was £0.28 million.   The revised estimate in June 1992 was £0.55 million.   The National Audit Office (NAO) commented "To gain the full benefits of the fast-track "design and build" contractual method it is essential that the user's requirements are carefully and fully defined at the outset.   In this case, because of deficiencies in the user's brief, which formed the basis of the investment appraisal, there were 13 contract variation orders covering additional requirements which almost doubled the cost and more than doubled the timescale".   The Public Accounts Committee reported "The Ministry told us that the lapses in control resulted partly from the project sponsors not having been appointed at the beginning of the project and partly because procedures were not sufficiently established at the time.   They also told us that the users of the New Glasshouse had not thought sufficiently about what they wanted and that revisions to the specification after the start of the contract had greatly increased the cost".   (Sources: "Ministry of Agriculture, Fisheries and Food, management of Works Services", report by the Comptroller and Auditor General, February 1993, page 32, and Fourth Report of the Committee of Public Accounts, Session 1993/4, December 1993, page vii, paragraph 5.)*

Recommendation 7: Co-ordinated Project Information

4.13 CPI is a technique which should have become normal practice years ago. In conjunction with the preparation of a full matrix of documents, its use should be made part of the conditions of engagement of the designers. If, as a result of the client's own instructions or through some problem on the part of the design team, the design drawings and specifications are not fully complete, and provisional sums are used, the consultants must make the client aware of the risks of incomplete design. The consultants should get specific approval through a "signing off" procedure, whereby the client is aware of the consequences for the construction programme in terms of possible cost and delay. Throughout the process, the emphasis must be on meeting the client's needs and keeping the client fully informed of potential risks.

Specialist Contractors and Design

4.14 The term "specialist contractor" can mean different things to different sections of the industry. Mr Martin Davis, in the Construction Management Forum Report and in his recent lecture to the SPIM Conference (see footnote 20 below), lists specialists as follows:-

Piling;	Heating and Ventilating Systems;
Structural Steelwork;	Air Conditioning;
Lifts and Escalators;	Hot and Cold Water Services;
Curtain walling and other forms of cladding;	Fire Engineering;
Flooring and suspended ceiling systems;	Public Health Engineering;
Information Technology and Communications networks;	Lighting and Power; Building automation, security and energy management systems.

4.15 These subdivide into two general categories:-

1. Those, such as curtain walling and lifts, which are basically **product orientated**, where the design input is responding to a performance specification, and where the skills of the specialist are in the quality, compliance, value for money and delivery of the product.

2. Those which are **systems orientated**, such as mechanical and electrical engineering services, who either carry out a design from inception, in response to a performance brief, or who work up the details of a conceptual design prepared by a consultant.

4.16 Many of the specialist engineering services may be provided by one specialist contractor employing other specialists in a subcontract capacity. This is particularly the case with mechanical and electrical (M&E) services. This section of the Report largely relates to their specialist role within the construction process.

4.17 The M&E contractors and consultants have played an active and valuable part in this Review. Their contributions to the construction industry are immense. The more complex the building, the higher is the likely value of the M&E input and the greater the design responsibility which will be passed by the architect/engineer to the building services consultant and the specialist contractor. In some projects, the value of the M&E content may exceed the builders' work.

4.18 The interface between consulting engineer and specialist engineering contractor can be problematic. The draft BSRIA report (see footnote 14) describes the "fuzzy edge disease" of the industry, and seeks to clarify the design responsibility between the two sets of specialists[18]. In general, the consulting engineer does the conceptual design and drawings and the specialist contractor is responsible for much of the detail, including necessary value engineering. The specialist contractors themselves often sub-let much of the installation work, such as ductwork, insulation, controls and sprinklers. Liability can involve complex legal questions, with the design consultant having to take "reasonable skill and care", whereas the installing specialist contractor may have a warranty which involves responsibility for "fitness for purpose".

4.19 The involvement of the consulting building services engineer/designer in the initial design process is essential. Few architects would claim to be specialists in the engineering services field. It is to be hoped that they will involve their other design colleagues in the planning and co-ordination of the project at the earliest stage. Greater difficulty can arise over the early involvement of specialist contractors, especially if they are expected to undertake significant detailed design responsibilities of their own. If they are taken on as domestic subcontractors by a main contractor post-tender, this may affect their ability to work directly in conjunction with the designers. The BSRIA report makes this point and adds that "having used the specialist's knowledge during the design process it is then logical that the same specialist would be appointed to carry out the works on site. This would enable the overall design to be completed with the necessary degree of certainty and would ensure that the site process could be properly planned and managed". The BSRIA report also comments that alternatively clients may prefer the specialist to be appointed post contract as a domestic subcontractor, and it makes some recommendations about how to integrate the specialist's design in those circumstances. Whatever the procurement route chosen by clients, the need to integrate and clarify design responsibilities remains.

4.20 There are several approaches available if the client does not wish the specialist to be engaged as a domestic subcontractor. They include:-

1. **Nomination**

   Many specialists (not only in the engineering services sector) would like the return of this system. But, as the SECG report points out, "only 11% of specialist engineering contractors are now nominated under JCT 80". (The percentage is higher in Northern Ireland.) Many clients do not wish to use this route. The CIPS final report describes the nomination system as "a contradiction in terms" and recommends that "the nomination system should be dropped"[19]. Since clients seem increasingly reluctant to use a long established procurement route which is available, I cannot recommend that it be followed as a normal procedure. But neither do I recommend its abolition.

---

[18] *Plant and equipment selection can also be a controversial area between consultant and specialist contractor.*

[19] *CIPS also points out that "The New Engineering Contract does not contain clauses allowing for nomination", and "neither German nor French contracts contain any provision".*

2. **Joint Ventures (JV)**

   Where high technology buildings have been commissioned, some general contractors and specialist engineering contractors have set up a joint company to undertake the work. This route is most effective where there is a large engineering services input, and the joint company can work satisfactorily on a basis of commercial equality. In such circumstances the general contractor tends to concentrate on managing the project and the M&E joint venture partner on providing the specialist engineering services. The joint company comes together as one single contractor. It is therefore suitable for design and build schemes, as well as contracts let upon the traditional basis. The SECG is concerned that the law on joint and several liability militates against JV arrangements. That problem is dealt with elsewhere in this report. The JV route can be a very effective one for the client, in that the specialist design input can be achieved at the earliest stage. It also provides continuing single joint responsibility for the client, who transfers to the general contractor and the specialist contractor jointly the responsibility to work together as a single corporate entity during the project. Some clients may be concerned about long term liabilities and how they will be discharged if a JV company is dissolved after completion of a contract, unless there are also continuing "parent guarantees".

3. **Separate Contracts**

   If the client wishes to deal separately with the specialist contractor, but does not wish to use either nomination or a joint venture route, it can let separate contracts.

4. **Construction Management**

   This is the most effective route for the client wishing to deal direct with specialist contractors (and trade contractors) of all kinds, and to create a clear contractual relationship with them. It also allows for full participation by the specialists in design and other commercial decisions from an early date. It is a tough system to manage, requiring considerable involvement by the client in conjunction with the construction manager. Not all clients will wish to accept the financial risks to which it can expose them. But some very successful projects have been brought to fruition under this procurement route. It is extensively used by some substantial clients. It is possible under the New Engineering Contract but not, as yet, under any JCT Form, though one is in preparation. This method also allows for a two stage pricing system if the design is incomplete at the time the specialist is appointed and a firm price cannot be established.[20]

5. **Appointing the Specialist as Main Contractor**

   Where the specialist work represents much of the value of the project, the client can employ the specialist contractor as main contractor, and pass to that firm the responsibilities of employing another firm to do the builder's work.

---

[20] *For details of the role of two stage pricing of specialist engineering work within construction management, see "Construction Management Forum, Report and Guidance" published by the Centre for Strategic Studies in Construction, Reading University, 1991, pages 62-67, the lecture given by Mr Martin Davis to the SPIM Conference on 25th March 1994 and the SECG final report.*

Recommendation 8: Allocation of M&E Design Responsibilities

4.21 Whatever procurement system a client employs, the allocation of design responsibilities between consulting engineer and specialist engineering contractor should follow the check list of guidance either as set out in the BSRIA report (when published) or as promulgated by the JCT (see recommendation 6). There should also be a separate design agreement for the specialist engineering contractor, involving a fee and a common standard of liability to that of the design consultant.

Building Work

5.1 Having assessed the need, decided upon risk acceptance and thereby chosen the most suitable procurement route and prepared the brief, the client is faced with a wide choice of Standard Forms of Contract for a building project. Most building work is undertaken under main contracts produced by the Joint Contracts Tribunal (JCT), though these are frequently amended.

Engineering Work

5.2 Civil engineering projects are usually undertaken under Institution of Civil Engineers (ICE) Conditions of Contract, either the 5th or 6th Editions, which have separate designer-led, and design and construct versions. There is also a civil engineering Minor Works Form. These ICE Conditions are produced by the Conditions of Contract Standing Joint Committee (CCSJC). Process Plant Engineering takes place under a variety of documents, some of them devised by clients themselves, but also those prepared by the Institute of Chemical Engineers (IChemE), involving a lump sum document ("the Red Book") and a reimbursable version ("the Green Book"). Where the main purpose of the work is the supply and/or erection of electrical, electronic and mechanical plant, Model Forms are published by the Institution of Mechanical Engineers (IMechE) and the Institution of Electrical Engineers (IEE) known as MF/1 (supply and erection) and MF/2 (supply only).

Government Work

5.3 A good deal of central Government work is procured under GC/Works/1, prepared and published by the DOE but also used by other Departments (sometimes with amendments). Some Government clients use their own contract, (such as the Department of Transport's design and construct form) or use Standard Forms such as ICE 5th or JCT 80 with their own amendments.

Other Contracts

5.4 The Interim Report mentioned various other contract documents. The New Engineering Contract (NEC) has recently (1993) been published by the Institution of Civil Engineers, and is already in use. The British Property Federation's System (1983) is not of itself widely used, but significant elements of it now appear in JCT 81 (With Contractor's Design). The general approach of the BPF System is also followed by the NEC. The SEACC procurement system, published initially by the Electrical Contractors' Association and since approved by the SECG, does not yet seem to have been taken up. But some of its features are increasingly favoured, and are recommended later in this Report.

Clients' Choice

5.5 The choice of contract conditions is a matter for the client, who arranges the funding for the project and/or pays for it. Where both main parties in the process - employer and contractor - are equally matched, the choice of contract conditions may be mutually agreed. In practice, market forces usually make one party dominant.

5.6 I have considered whether the recommendations made later in this Report - and especially those involving legislation set out in Chapter 8 - should also apply to work covered by IChemE and I MechE/IEE contract documents. No detailed concern has been expressed to the Review by the process plant sector. However, I note that some process plant clients, particularly in the water and power industries, already use the NEC and/or have joined the NEC Users' Group. It is possible that other process plant clients may wish to use this contract, with its emphasis on teamwork. The Implementation Forum proposed in Chapter 12 should consider further, prior to the drafting of the legislation, whether the process plant sector should be covered by it.

5.7 I have received a great deal of evidence about the Standard JCT and ICE Forms and domestic subcontracts which are designed to accompany them (such as DOM/1 and the "Blue Form"). Their reception is mixed and, in practice, many significant public and private clients and contractors either heavily amend or do not use the Standard Forms. This suggests that the time has come for a fresh look at the issue.

Survey Findings

5.8 Two surveys relating to the subject of this Review have produced interesting findings. Both were conducted as part of the series of the "New Builder"/JT Design Build attitude surveys. The first, during September 1993, involved a panel of 150 major companies including public and private sector clients, civil engineering contractors, materials manufacturers, subcontractors, general building contractors and professional consultants.

1. The sample considered that the main strengths of the contractual arrangements were that they were well known/established (58%) and fair (42%).

2. The main weaknesses were listed as encouraging conflict/litigation (52%), insufficiently clear (45%) and created a high level of mistrust (38%).

3. When asked to list their three most important changes to improve the general efficiency and productivity of the industry, the second most popular choice (40%) was for "simpler contracts (e.g. the New Engineering Contract) - especially for small sized projects".

(Source: New Builder, 1 October 1993.)

5.9 A further survey took place under the same auspices in March 1994. On this occasion a panel of 180 major companies was approached. Respondents were asked how the arrangements for risk apportionment within the contractual frame work could be improved. The results are shown in table 4 (with multiple answers being given). A question was also asked about the Joint Contracts Tribunal (the results are shown in table 5). 10 of the 33 clients polled were in the public sector, and 5 of them were from local authorities.

TABLE 4

In your opinion how could the arrangements for "risk" apportionment within the contractual framework be improved?

		All Respondents
1.	(Further) Standardisation of contractual documentation	52%
2.	More openness by parties involved on where main risks may occur at the beginning of project	42%
3.	More equitable risk/reward apportionment built into contracts	36%
4.	Develop a "partnership" approach to apportioning risk	32%
5.	Introduction of independent adjudicators (person not employed by either client or contractor)	28%
6.	(Majority of) Risk to be appointed to a single party only	15%

TABLE 5

How far do you agree with the statement that "the Joint Contracts Tribunal (JCT) provides a good service for the industry and its clients"?

	Contractors	Consultants	Clients
Strongly Agree	13%	15%	12%
Slightly Agree	61%	42%	28%
Neither	14%	20%	32%
Slightly Disagree	12%	15%	20%
Strongly Disagree	-%	8%	8%

Source: New Builder/JT Construction Industry Attitude Survey, March 1994.

5.10 Bonds have long been a controversial part of the construction process. The Secretary of State for the Environment announced in a speech last November that the DOE would prepare guidelines to apply throughout Government on the use of bonds. He was critical of on-demand bonds, as are the CIEC. Bonds are intended to be a protection against failure or poor performance. As this DOE work is in progress, I do not need to duplicate it. But I believe that the DOE's guidance on bonds should be formulated within these principles:-

1. They should be drafted in comprehensible and modern language.

2. They should not be on-demand and unconditional, but should have clearly defined circumstances set out in them for being called.

3. If the circumstances/conditions provided for in the bond are fulfilled, the beneficiary should be able to obtain prompt payment without recourse to litigation.

4. They should have a clear end date.

"Pay When Paid" Clauses - Government Conditions

5.11 Recent action, and discussion, has necessarily worked within the existing system. The DOE has circulated guidance to Departments about amending the Standard Forms of Contract. The aim is to reinforce the payment arrangements relating to subcontractors which are set out in subcontract documents in normal use such DOM/1 or GW/S. The Constructors Liaison Group (CLG) and other subcontractor groups such as the Confederation of Construction Specialists strongly support this action. Indeed, they want the Government to go faster and further and introduce legislation to ban "pay when paid" clauses, and also to impose penal interest rates on late payments[21]. Conversely, the CIEC is very unhappy about the DOE guidance. It believes that the 17 day standard period under DOM/1, within which domestic subcontractors in building are supposed to be paid, is now too short. It argues that the client has up to 14 days after receiving the architect's certificate to pay one cheque to a main contractor, but the main contractor may have dozens of subcontractors to pay. The CIEC proposes instead in its final report that a 30 day payment period for subcontractors should be substituted, and adds that if that were to happen many larger contractors would be more willing to use forms such as DOM/1. It also advocates that clients should honour architects' certificates within 7 days. It accepts that:-

a   If payment is delayed by the client due to some failure of the main contractor or some other subcontractor, the "innocent" subcontractors should be still paid by the main contractor.

b   If the client becomes insolvent, the main contractor should still pay the domestic subcontractors in full, but nominated or named subcontractors would have to share some of the risks of the client's insolvency with the main contractor.

[21] *The White Paper "Competitiveness - Helping Business to Win", HMSO, May 1994, spells out new duties of prompt payment for Government Departments and Agencies and proposes a further package of additional measures but without legislation. However, the White Paper adds that if there has not been a "significant improvement" in the next 2 years, the case for legislation will be reviewed.*

The CIEC argues that "pay when paid clauses" should continue. It states that if a 30 day payment period for subcontractors was introduced in domestic subcontracts, it would then consider supporting a contractual right to interest on late payments, as already exists in ICE Conditions, provided a similar right was also available under the main contract.

5.12   These proposed changes only affect contracts placed by Government Departments. They reflect a willingness to meet strongly held views of some participants in the construction process. I can entirely understand, and sympathise with, the Government's wish to reinforce the payment arrangements, which are supposed to be standard within the industry in any case. But such new clauses seek, in a real sense, damage limitation within a controversial system. They do not go to the core of the problem, which is the reluctance of many participants to abide by, or even use, current Standard Forms, without amendment. There are many alterations to such Standard Forms which have been suggested to the Review. I believe we need to step back from such proposals and ask a more fundamental question. Is it possible to create a new framework within which contracts will be more acceptable and thereby left unchanged? Endlessly refining the existing forms has taken place for decades, frequently to accommodate decisions of the Courts. Such refinements have not provided an acceptable outcome. They are still too easily deleted or amended, or an "in-house" contract substituted. All this activity detracts from the real business of construction and results in energies being focused on procedures rather than production.

Thinking the Problem Through Again

5.13   There are several ways to approach the concerns expressed by all sides of the construction process about contracts. They are:-

1. To do nothing.

2. To amend existing Standard Forms to meet some of the concerns.

3. To try to define what a modern construction contract ought to contain. If this can be achieved, there are then two further alternatives, which are to change existing contract forms to take account of such requirements, and/or to introduce a new contract which will deliver them.

5.14   It is no longer possible to do nothing. That option can be discarded at once.

5.15   Before choosing alternatives, it is desirable to ask some basic questions:

1. Are there too many forms of contract? Or too few? Does the number matter?

2. Are some of them inherently adversarial, or likely to produce conflict because of the modern structure of the industry?

3. Are there some procurement routes which are more likely to produce a result which meets the client's wishes, and which should therefore be followed? If so, which?

4. Are there certain features which should be adopted across the range of contacts?

5. Are there any contracts which should be used more often?

5.16 There are no universally acceptable answers to any of those questions. There is a vast literature on the industry's contract documentation. There are many courses of learned lectures available. Thousands of highly experienced practitioners have worked for decades in drafting, administering and sitting in judgement upon the contracts. Some believe that a contract which is not negotiated through the industry's established procedures (the JCT or the CCSJC) will not achieve acceptance. But equally, there are those who take the view that such documents do not meet their commercial requirements. These issues are not ultimately susceptible of resolution through scientific analysis. In any case, contracts exist to serve the construction process, not vice versa. During successful projects the contract document is "left in the drawer".

5.17 In paragraph 5.15, I posed five questions about contracts. My personal answers are:-

1. The number of available contracts is not significant. Clients should choose the procurement route which best suits their purpose, and use the appropriate form of contract.

2. Contracts which are drafted on the basis that:

    a. design and construction are totally separated, in that the main contractor and subcontractors have no design responsibilities or involvement in the preparation of the design;

    b. all design work will be fully planned by consultants retained by the client and not subject to change once tender information has been sent out;

    c. the actual construction work will mainly be carried out by the contractor rather than by domestic subcontractors;

    d. the architect or engineer acting as contract administrator will also be accepted by the parties to the main contract as impartial adjudicator between client and contractor, especially over matters relating to measurement and certification of work done and related payment or time issues;

    do not seem to me to relate easily to reality on modern construction sites and may require revision or replacement by other contractual approaches.

3. Contracts which best meet client objectives on procurement may involve modules which can be adapted by mutual agreement to the particular project. Putting the modules into a standard format means that the system brings together flexibility and familiarity.

4. Certain common features are desirable. They should include:-

    a. A general duty to trade fairly, with specific requirements relating to payment and related issues;

    b. clearly defined work stages, including milestones or other forms of activity schedule;

    c. the pre-pricing of any variations;

    d. an adjudication system which is independent of contract administration.

5. The approach of the New Engineering Contract is extremely attractive.[22]

5.18 The most effective form of contract in modern conditions should include:-

1. A specific duty for all parties to deal fairly with each other, and with their subcontractors, specialists and suppliers, in an atmosphere of mutual co-operation.

2. Firm duties of teamwork, with shared financial motivation to pursue those objectives. These should involve a general presumption to achieve "win-win" solutions to problems which may arise during the course of the project.

3. A wholly interrelated package of documents which clearly defines the roles and duties of all involved, and which is suitable for all types of project and for any procurement route.

4. Easily comprehensible language and with Guidance Notes attached.

5. Separation of the roles of contract administrator, project or lead manager and adjudicator. The Project or lead Manager should be clearly defined as client's representative.

6. A choice of allocation of risks, to be decided as appropriate to each project but then allocated to the party best able to manage, estimate and carry the risk.

7. Taking all reasonable steps to avoid changes to pre-planned works information. But, where variations do occur, they should be priced in advance, with provision for independent adjudication if agreement cannot be reached.

8. Express provision for assessing interim payments by methods other than monthly valuation i.e. mile stones, activity schedules or payment schedules. Such arrangements must also be reflected in the related subcontract documentation. The eventual aim should be to phase out the traditional system of monthly measurement or remeasurement but meanwhile provision should still be made for it.

9. Clearly setting out the period within which interim payments must be made to all participants in the process, failing which they will have an automatic right to compensation, involving payment of interest at a sufficiently heavy rate to deter slow payment.

10. Providing for secure trust fund routes of payment.

11. While taking all possible steps to avoid conflict on site, providing for speedy dispute resolution if any conflict arises, by a pre-determined impartial adjudicator/referee/expert.

12. Providing for incentives for exceptional performance.

13. Making provision where appropriate for advance mobilisation payments (if necessary, bonded) to contractors and subcontractors, including in respect of off-site prefabricated materials provided by part of the construction team.

---

22 *The NEC Users' Group was launched in January 1994. Its first Newsletter (Spring 1994) says that "more than 700 contracts have been let under the NEC around the world". As of the 3 March 1994, BAA plc. had already used it on 13 contracts. 11 of them are civil engineering and infrastructure works and the other two are building schemes. They range in value from £0.75 million to over £60 million, and total over £100 million. All the contracts have made provision for a named adjudicator, but in no case has it been necessary to call upon the service of the adjudicator, because the Project Manager and the contractor have agreed matters between themselves. (Source: Letter from Mr Michael Maine, Group Technical Director, BAA plc, 3 March 1994.)*

TABLE 6: PAYMENT TIMES UNDER MAJOR STANDARD FORMS

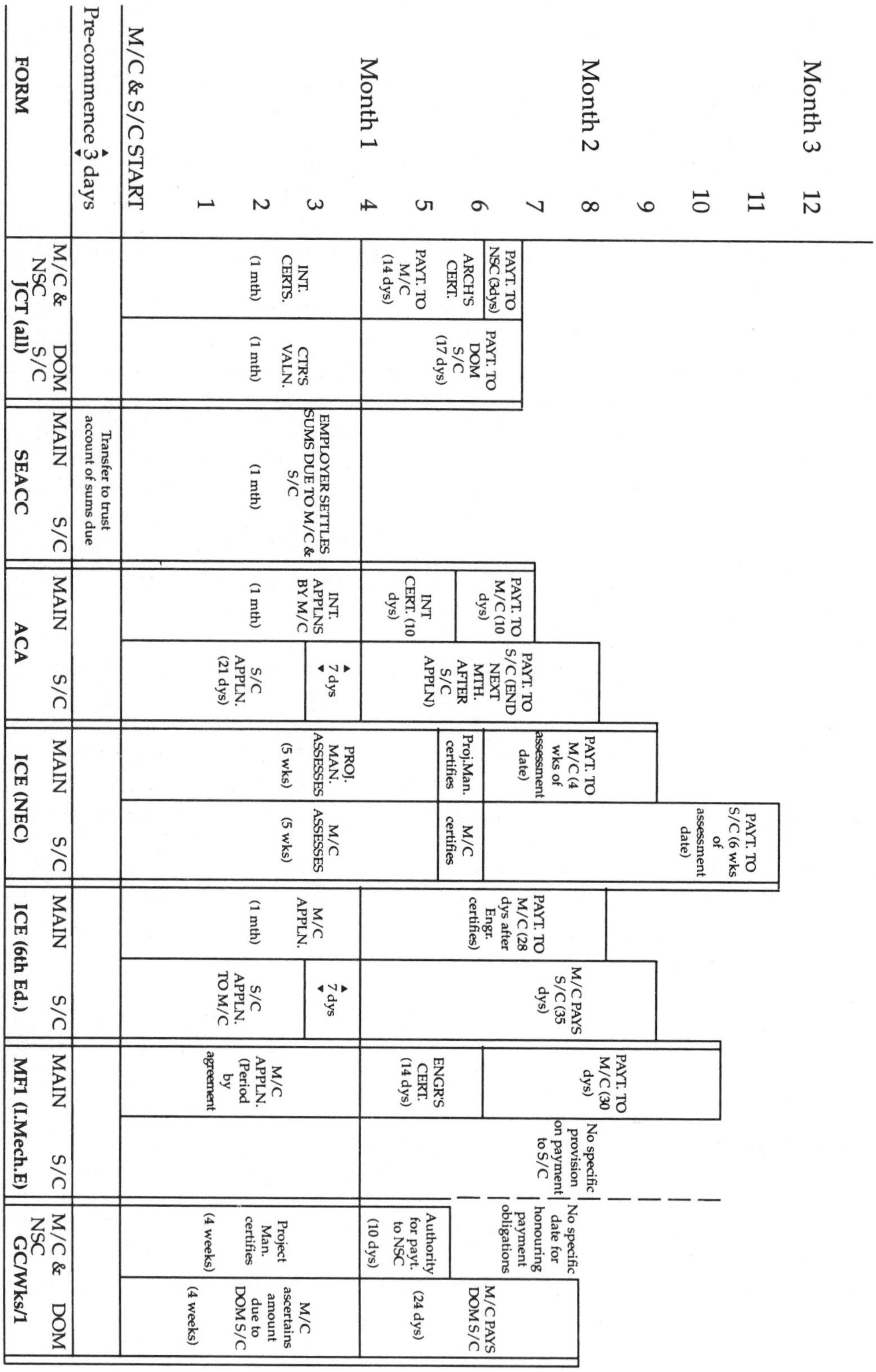

The following is a timeline (Gantt-style) chart, read with the time axis running from "Pre-commence 3 days" and "M/C & S/C START" through Month 1 (weeks 1–6), Month 2 (weeks 7–8) and Month 3 (weeks 9–12). Each FORM is split into a MAIN (M/C & NSC) row and an S/C (DOM S/C) row.

FORM	Row	Entries (with durations)
JCT (all)	M/C & NSC	PAYT. TO NSC (3 days); ARCH'S CERT.; PAYT. TO M/C (14 dys); INT. CERTS. (1 mth)
	DOM S/C	PAYT. TO DOM S/C (17 dys); CTRS VALN. (1 mth)
SEACC	MAIN	EMPLOYER SETTLES SUMS DUE TO M/C & S/C (1 mth)
	S/C	Transfer to trust account of sums due
ACA	MAIN	PAYT. TO M/C (10 dys); INT CERT. (10 dys); INT. APPLNS BY M/C (1 mth)
	S/C	PAYT. TO S/C (END NEXT MTH. AFTER S/C APPLN); 7 dys; S/C APPLN. (21 dys)
ICE (NEC)	MAIN	PAYT. TO M/C (4 wks of assessment date); Proj.Man. certifies; PROJ. MAN. ASSESSES (5 wks)
	S/C	PAYT. TO S/C (6 wks of assessment date); M/C certifies; M/C ASSESSES (5 wks)
ICE (6th Ed.)	MAIN	PAYT. TO M/C (28 dys after Engr. certifies); Engr. certifies; M/C APPLN. (1 mth)
	S/C	M/C PAYS S/C (35 dys); 7 dys; S/C APPLN. TO M/C
MF1 (I.Mech.E)	MAIN	PAYT. TO M/C (30 dys); ENGR'S CERT. (14 dys); M/C APPLN. (Period by agreement)
	S/C	No specific date for honouring payment obligations; No specific provision on payment to S/C
GC/Wks/1	M/C & NSC	M/C PAYS DOM S/C; Authority for payt. to NSC (24 dys); Project Man. certifies; M/C ascertains amount due to DOM S/C (10 dys)
	DOM S/C	(4 weeks); (4 weeks)

Time axis markers:
- Pre-commence 3 days
- M/C & S/C START
- Month 1: 1, 2, 3, 4, 5, 6
- Month 2: 7, 8
- Month 3: 9, 10, 11, 12

Source: SECG, prepared for the Review

5.19 The New Engineering Contract contains virtually all of these assumptions of best practice, and others, which are set out in the Core Clauses, the main and secondary options.

5.20 There are some alterations which I believe ought to be made to the NEC to bring it fully within those principles.

1. Its name should be changed, since it can equally be used for building projects. I suggest the "New Construction Contract".

2. Provision should made, as a Core Clause, for a secure trust fund to be arranged, into which the client deposits payments for each milestone, activity schedule or interim payment period before the commencement of the relevant period. This will provide much greater confidence for contractors and subcontractors.

3. Subcontractors have expressed concern about the potential length of payment times under the NEC procedures. These concerns are set out in Table 6 prepared by the SECG. They suggest that payments to subcontractors could be up to 3 months after work has been carried out by them. However, the objective under the NEC is to pay both contractor and subcontractor from the assessment date rather than from the certificate date. The authors of the NEC believe that this gives protection to both main contractors and subcontractors. It is also the case that the NEC is drafted to facilitate payment on a 4-4-5 week cycle and the normal payment interval is expected to be one month. The NEC also allows for a construction management procurement route (with no main contractor), and late payment automatically attracts a right of interest (Clause 51.2, NEC subcontract). I recommend however that the payment periods be reviewed in conjunction with clients, contractors and subcontractors. This may allow for agreement on an alternative timescale which is acceptable to all.

4. A statement should be written into Core Clause 1 that the employer and the contractor affirm that they both intend to establish a fair and reasonable agreement with each other to undertake the project in a spirit of mutual trust and co-operation, and to trade fairly with each other and with their subcontractors and suppliers. Core Clause 16.3 should be strengthened to make it clear that "win-win" solutions to problems will be devised in a spirit of partnership. Identical wording should be included in the appropriate Core Clauses in the subcontract document.

5. Core Clause 1 in both main and subcontract documents should contain an express provision that none of the Core Clauses will be amended by either party to the contract. It should be a mandatory condition of the Core Clauses that the main contractor will only use the NEC subcontract in employing any subcontractor when using a formal document[23] and will not amend any of the Core Clauses. They should only include those main and secondary options which are contained in the main contract, unless both parties agree to changes in the options in the subcontract document. Subcontractors should accept similar restrictions on their contractual dealings with sub subcontractors. If this spirit of co-operation which the NEC wishes to foster is achieved, such provisions should in practice be unnecessary. But in the present adversarial atmosphere, and with the need to change deep rooted cultural attitudes, it will add to confidence if they are included.

---

[23] *This is designed to meet the case where subcontractors are retained for small jobs, for example, on a labour only basis.*

6. A full matrix of consultants' and adjudicators' terms of appointment should be published, interlocked with the main contract. (These are currently in draft.) Standard tender documents and bonds would also be desirable. The adjudication procedures may need some amendment to bring them within the principles of Chapter 9 of this Report.

7. Provision should be made for a simpler and shorter minor works document.[24]

Existing Contracts

5.21 It is possible for the industry and clients to continue with the existing JCT and ICE Forms. Many may wish to do so, at least at present, because they are used to them. But, if so, I would strongly recommend that the existing forms be amended to take account of the principles set out in paragraph 5.18 above. My sixth principle, a choice of risks, is met in the JCT/ICE families through a variety of contracts rather than through the NEC's Core Clauses and options. I believe that the approach of the contract drafting committees, and their composition, needs to be changed, and I make recommendations accordingly later in this Chapter and in Appendix 4. Despite recommendations from some participants, I have not been prepared to recommend statutory intervention to impose the present contracts or subcontracts upon any parties to the process. That would not have been a realistic approach when those contracts themselves were controversial. But I believe that if the contracts - whether through use of an amended NEC or by changing the JCT/ICE documents - do meet the principles of this Chapter, it will then be appropriate to legislate to support them. If generally acceptable contracts have come into use, there will no longer be any need to use "bespoke" contracts or to impose unilateral and onerous conditions driven by greater commercial power. The law will reinforce agreed best practice, rather than being burdensome or unreasonable to one of the parties.

The Contract Committees

5.22 I turn now to consider the existing building and civil engineering industry committees dealing with contract conditions. Some evidence to the Review has called for the abolition of one or both of them.

5.23 The two committees charged with delivering the Standard Forms of Contract - the JCT and the CCSJC - are separate. The Banwell Committee in 1964 recommended that there should be one single joint contract form for building and civil engineering. That was rejected by a joint meeting of the JCT and the Joint Contracts Committee (now the CCSJC) as a "doctrinaire objective". However, the Economic Development Committee (EDC) for Civil Engineering in its commentary on Banwell in 1968 ("Contracting in Civil Engineering Since Banwell") and the equivalent report of the EDC for Building in 1967 ("Action on the Banwell Report") were much less dismissive. But no joint contract has been devised by the two committees. The ICE 5th and 6th conditions have both been published since the Banwell Report. The Department of Transport, which is the largest single procurer for civil engineering work, uses ICE 5th (with amendments). It has also introduced its own design and construct contract, with no direct involvement of the CCSJC. The Scottish Office Roads Department, another substantial procurer, has introduced its

---

[24] *For example, the Landscape Institute regards the NEC as too complex even for landscape services in connection with civil engineering projects (evidence, April 1994).*

Alternative Tender Initiative, which appears to be highly successful in its out-turn results but drew initial criticism from some sections of the industry for its transference of risk. The ICE, which is a constituent party to the CCSJC, has produced the New Engineering Contract. While there was extensive public discussion of the NEC, the working party which prepared it over 8 years did not work within the confines of the CCSJC.

5.24 The CCSJC itself has an interesting structure. Contractors are represented through the FCEC and consultant engineers through the ACE. But clients are represented through the Institution of Civil Engineers, which is a learned society embracing individual civil engineers in all kinds of employment or self-employment. It is not an organisation of clients as such. There is no direct representation of subcontractors on the CCSJC. It is a source of grievance to subcontractors that while the Federation of Associations of Specialists and Subcontractors (FASS) and the Confederation of Associations of Specialist Engineering Contractors (CASEC) "approved" the "Blue" FCEC subcontract form linked to ICE 5th, they were not invited by the FCEC to do the same for the amended version to go with the 6th edition. The amendments to the "Blue Form" were not controversial. They consisted of stepping down the changes made to the main contract. The reason why the subcontractors were not involved appears to have been that it took 10 years to reach agreement on the 5th edition's "Blue Form". The FCEC was apparently concerned that the subcontractors would insist upon re-opening wider debate upon the whole "Blue Form" if they were consulted about the changes to the 6th edition version.

5.25 I believe that the time is now ripe for radical changes to the JCT and the CCSJC. I consider each of them in turn.

Recommendation 9: The Joint Contracts Tribunal

5.26 I do not favour disbanding the Joint Contracts Tribunal. It has existed for 63 years, and has support within the building industry. However, it should make its structure more relevant to modern conditions within the industry. The representation of clients is inadequate in the private sector and is disproportionate for the modern procurement role of local authorities. I recommend that:

1. **Structure:** The structure is changed so that it is subdivided into units which reflect the actual parties to the specific agreements or contracts, who should then draw up their own documents. It makes little sense for interests who are not actually parties to a particular document to obstruct changes in it for reasons which may be unconnected with the proposed change, or even with the document itself.

2. **Family of Documents:** A complete family of standard documents is produced based on the principles in paragraph 5.18. This should include a total matrix of interlocking consultants' agreements and contracts, including subcontracts, available for all kinds of building work, and any additional relevant documentation such as bonds and warranties (if necessary) and latent defects insurance. This can best be achieved by building on the NEC (as amended), in conjunction with the ICE which publishes it and holds the copyright. If, additionally, clients wish to continue to use current JCT documents, they should be redrafted to incorporate the principles in paragraph 5.18, be in comprehensible language and have guidance notes attached to them. To complete the family, other documents will have to be introduced or incorporated.

5.27 Further details of the recommended restructuring of the JCT are set out in Appendix IV. These changes are urgent. They should not await the legislative changes proposed elsewhere in the Report.

Recommendation 10: The CCSJC

5.28 The publication (and growing use) of the NEC and the introduction by the DOT and the Scottish Office Roads Department of their own design and construct contract forms or variant amendments also present new opportunities for civil engineering. The CCSJC should also change.

1. **Structure:** Clients should be directly represented by nominees from the proposed Construction Clients' Forum. Subcontractors should also be directly involved and represented. More details of the recommended changes are set out in Appendix IV.

2. **Family of Documents:** A complete family of documents should be produced based on the principles in paragraph 5.18. It should include a total matrix of interlocking consultants' agreements and contracts, including subcontracts and any additional relevant documentation such as bonds and warranties (if necessary). This can best be achieved by building upon the NEC (as amended). There should be close co-ordination with the restructured JCT (see paragraph 5.29). If, additionally, some clients wish to continue to use current ICE documents, they should be redrafted to incorporate the principles in paragraph 5.18. To complete the family, other documents will have to be introduced or incorporated.

Recommendation 11: Joint Liaison Committee

5.29 The JCT and CCSJC should co-ordinate their work. A Joint Liaison Committee should be formed to consider amendments to the NEC and to build up a complete family of documents around it. The NEC is capable of being a common contract for the whole industry. The JCT and the CCSJC should eventually merge into a National Construction Contracts Council.

Recommendations 12.1 - 12.2: Clients

5.30

1. Government Departments should undertake some contracts under the New Engineering Contract as soon as possible to gain experience in using it. The DOE should provide advice to other public sector agencies on the contract, and the range of options suitable for use. A target should be set of one third of Government funded projects started over the next four years to use the NEC. Departments which have been using GC/Works/1 or their own contracts should begin to change to the NEC. Any special conditions which they need to add relating to security, prevention of corruption or of discrimination can be included under option U of the NEC. It would, however, be desirable if they were in a standard format. It will also be open to them to use JCT or ICE Forms, as amended to meet the principles of paragraph 5.18.

2. Use of the NEC (as amended) by private sector clients should be strongly promoted by client and industry bodies.

6.1 The Interim Report sought to identify 5 different issues:-

1. Professional consultants should be selected on a basis which properly recognises quality as well as price.

2. The need for a lead manager.

3. Contractors should not be required to undergo excessive or burdensome qualification procedures.

4. Tender lists - including those for design and build projects - should be of a sensible length.

5. Value for money and future cost-in-use should play an important part in the selection process.

Competitive Fees

6.2 It is now widely - if in some quarters reluctantly - accepted among consultants that competitive fees are a permanent feature of their work. While I have received suggestions that consultants should return to compulsory fixed fee scales published by their professional Institutions, that is not regarded as realistic by many professionals themselves, let alone by other parts of the construction process. The Construction Industry Council, in its policy statement "Competing for Quality" (December 1992) states that "Professional fee scales are no longer relevant or appropriate"[25]. The Council's basic preference is for fees to be negotiated between client and professional consultant. The CIC added that, if a competition route is to be followed, it should involve a proper prequalification process to ensure that firms of equivalent capability, capacity and skill for the project are invited to tender. There should then be clear procedures for inviting, opening, assessing and awarding tenders. The CIC asked the Government to require public authorities to follow such procedures.

6.3 In his reply[26] to the Chairman of the CIC, Mr Ian Dixon CBE, on 12 February 1993, the then Secretary of State the Environment, Mr Michael Howard, made the following points:-

1. The procurement of professional services was not amenable to one system. Local authorities who were being required to introduce Compulsory Competitive Tendering (CCT) for professional services should be allowed flexibility.

---

[25] *"The Procurement of Professional Services", published by Thomas Telford Services Limited on behalf of the CIC, 1993. The policy statement "Competing for Quality" is on pages 2 & 3.*

[26] *Letter from the Rt. Hon. Michael Howard QC, MP.*

2. The Government could not accept negotiation as the main route, though it might be suitable in some circumstances.

3. Government policy was based on the premise that competition was the best way to achieve value for money. But price had never been the sole criterion. Quality judgements were recognised as an "essential part of good procurement practice".

4. He expected Government Departments to review the effectiveness of recent competitive fees "as a matter of course". The Central Unit on Procurement also maintained an overview of project costs.

5. The Department, and other public sector clients, were involved in a study of the issue by the Construction Industry Research and Information Association (CIRIA). They were in discussion with Local Authority Associations and others about how to implement CCT.

6.4 Government Accounting and the Government's "Public Purchasing Policy: Consolidated Guidelines" have also made clear that value for money, not lowest price, should be the aim. This was endorsed in the White Paper "Competitiveness - Helping Business to Win" (HMSO, May 1994). This is an area of policy where it is difficult to assess the effects. Few professional consultants are likely to admit openly that they have personally reduced their services because of competitive fees. Such competition is now extremely widespread. A survey published by "New Builder", (25 March 1994), of 327 professional services firms found that 39% of firms currently earn more than 70% of their commissions on a competitive fee basis. The equivalent figure for 1991 was 14%. Conversely, the proportion of firms negotiating more than 70% of their commissions has fallen from 55% in 1991 to 29% in 1994. This trend continued during 1993, a period in which market conditions showed some improvement for professional consultants, suggesting that clients now expect this to be the normal procurement route. Some well known firms in the survey were reportedly obtaining over 80% or even 90% of their work through competitive fees.

6.5 Since many firms have adapted their approaches to winning work to involve competitive fees, it might be thought that events had overtaken the concerns of the CIC. But there are some thought provoking comments from firms of architects in the report of the RIAS entitled "Value or Cost" (op.cit.). For example:-

1. "Much of their work is done as a technical loss ....Divisions in plan of work are crumbling. Will fight to minimise investment, visits to site will be limited and there is a fortnightly cost control meeting. Number of production drawings cut by 30%."

2. "We look to limit our service in the fee tendered service and are prepared to claim for extra services. We only make the client aware when appropriate. We cut back on [stages] A to D, and severely limit service after [stage] G, and are ready to claim for any additional efforts. We cut down on meetings/site visits/ number of drawings and manufacturer's drawings. We do not do site minutes, we design it only once, and alterations will be on time."

3. "The fee tendered service may not exclude any of what used to be included in a normal service, but may alter depth, and probably rule out record drawings".

6.6 A recent survey[27] by the Association of Consulting Engineers (ACE) found:-

a. 73% give less consideration to design alternatives;

---

[27] *The ACE surveyed 68 of its members who were representative in terms of size and discipline. 53 questionnaires were returned, of which one was discarded.*

b. 31% give less consideration to checking and reviewing designs;

c. 40% consider that the risks of design errors occurring are higher;

d. 74% admit that they are producing simpler designs to minimise the commitment of resources to a task;

e. 60% consider that capital costs of construction and operation are higher as a result of (d);

f. 84% assess the number of claims for additional fees to be higher;

g. 33% thought the frequency of problems on site are higher;

h. 49% said the frequency of visits to site are lower;

i. 29% said they pay less attention to environmental concerns;

j. 12% pay less attention to health and safety both in design and on the site;

k. 67% resist client changes to designs;

l. 69% see less trust between client and consulting engineer;

m. 79% are spending less resources on training graduates and technicians;

n. 77% are spending less resources on Continuing Professional Development training and courses;

o. 75% are spending less time on the writing of professional papers;

p. 56% are devoting less time to professional activities;

q. 94% bid low to maintain the cash flow or (on occasion) to test the market;

r. 35% bid low with the intention of doing less than in the enquiry;

s. 61% bid low with the intention of making up fees with claim for variations.

(Source: ACE evidence, May 1994)

6.7   The selection arrangements of Government Departments vary. The DOE has a register of consultants (ConReg). As of 23 February 1994, there were 3239 names on it[28]. Other Departments such as the Ministry of Defence (MOD) and the Department of Transport (DOT) have their own databases for consultants (only for Project Managers in the case of MOD). The MOD (Defence Works Services) retains a Project Manager (PM) through a competitive tendering system involving two envelopes, and it is the PM's responsibility to retain the other consultants and to pay their fees. Both MOD (whose processes are currently under review) and the DOT give some weight to quality considerations[29].

---

[28] *Parliamentary Answer by Mr Tony Baldry MP, Hansard, 23 February 1994, Written Answers Col 262. See also a separate answer from Mr Baldry on 9 March (Hansard Column 296) regarding the use by other departments of CMIS and ConReg. Both replies were to Mr John Spellar MP.*

[29] *"Obtaining quality and value through competition in the procurement of professional services - Research Report", (currently unpublished) by Davis, Langdon and Everest for CIRIA.*

6.8 Clients have the right to expect the highest possible commitment to their project from their consultants. They should also know in advance how much they will have to pay for a full service or, if they want a restricted service, what it will involve and how much it will cost[30]. Government Departments should give a lead to the public sector, and hopefully also influence private clients by their example.

6.9 There is a need for an objective and generally accepted system which will allow a proper qualitative as well as price assessment of consultant bids for creative professional services. Such objective criteria are essential for public sector procurers, in assessing value for money and in convincing public auditors that they have pursued a clear and defensible route in their choice of consultants. The National Audit Office have indicated that the selection of tenders other than the lowest in the wider interests of value for money is acceptable[31]. There is a strong case for public sector clients to justify the appointment of any consultant on value for money grounds irrespective of whether they are the lowest bid. The Central Unit on Procurement Guidance Note no 13 "The Selection and Appointment of Works Consultants" also stresses the need to choose the best consultant teams, based on past proven performance, qualifications, experience, competence and availability of resource, and involving a prequalification system. It also warns against accepting a tender which will result in the consultants undertaking the work at a loss[32].

6.10 At least three organisations are currently involved in preparing such detailed objective criteria for assessing quality as well as price. They have shown me their documents, either complete or in draft. They are:-

1. The Association of Consulting Engineers, which has already published "Balancing Quality and Price - Value Assessment and the Selection of Consulting Engineers".

2. The CIC, which as this Report went to press, was about to publish its own document entitled "Guidance for the Value Assessment of Competitive Tenders".

3. CIRIA, which is still considering a draft guide prepared for it by Davis, Langdon and Everest Consultancy Group, following extensive research of current practice in both the public and private sectors.

A consultation paper was issued in February 1994 by DOE relating to the extension of Compulsory Competitive Tendering to local authorities' construction related services. This suggests that it is for local authorities to make decisions on the appropriate balance between price and quality in evaluating tenders under CCT. The Local Government Management Board, on behalf of the Local Authority Associations, published guidance on assessment of quality in the application of CCT in March 1994. Neither document contains a numerical method of assessing quality, unlike those listed above, and were not intended to do so.

---

[30] *In that regard, the Ground Forum has recommended:-*

(1) *consulting engineers bidding for a commission should specify either their in-house expertise on geotechnical engineering, or how they intend to obtain it; and*

(2) *universal compliance with the National Site Investigation Specification. (Evidence, April 1994)*

The Review has not been able to examine these specific proposals in the time available, but they should be considered by the task force recommended in paragraph 6.11 (5).

[31] *"We take the view that the selection of tenders other than the lowest is acceptable as long as the reasons for the choice are clearly and convincingly stated". NAO memorandum of 4 December 1992, reprinted in "British Construction; in pursuit of excellence" by Clive Priestley CB, published by the Business Round Table 1994, page 41.*

[32] *See paragraph 9.1 to 9.7 of CUP 13 (which is currently being updated by the CUP).*

6.11 I recommend:-

1. A register based on ConReg should be compiled of consultant firms seeking public sector work in the United Kingdom, to be kept by the DOE. Consultants not seeking public sector work would not need to register.

2. Local authorities and other public bodies should be strongly encouraged to make use of ConReg, rather than keeping their own registers.

3. The aim should be that public sector work should be restricted to consultant firms who are on ConReg, which should be regularly reviewed. Firms applying to go on the register should be required to demonstrate some appropriate professional and managerial skills, the availability of resources and adequate professional indemnity insurance.

4. A charge should be levied on those firms joining the register to help defray the cost to public funds.

5. A small task force should be set up by the DOE in conjunction with other public and private clients and the CIC, to choose and then endorse a specific quality and price assessment mechanism for the engagement of professional consultants. The chosen route should then be set out in the CSCP. The task force may also wish to consider other detailed issues related to prequalification of consultants and the development of ConReg.

Lead Manager or Project Manager

6.12 The Interim Report found "widespread acceptance amongst consultants that a lead manager should always be appointed for the design process, to head an integrated design team". This in the past was the traditional role of the architect or engineer. Because of the complexity of modern construction techniques, it has become increasingly difficult for designers to be responsible for all aspects of design of a large project, and also act as contract administrators. Clients have looked for a single person/firm to pull the whole process together for them. They have tended to go through a number of stages. The first is to seek one leader of the consultants' team, who may not be the principal designer. The second is to ask the leader to be responsible for advising upon the appointment of the other consultants. The next stage is for the leader to become the channel between the client and the contractor. From there it is only a small step to becoming a single Project Manager who is responsible, as the representative of the client, for dealing with the contractor and the other consultants. Some forms of contract such as the New Engineering Contract and the BPF System recognise the Project Manager (or client's representative) as the specific representative of the employer.

6.13 Every project has to be managed. But that does not necessarily require a separate or external Project Manager (PM). Many well-instructed clients have their own in house Project Management. Conversely, some Government Departments, and especially the Ministry of Defence Works Services, retain external PMs by advertisement and competitive fees for most of their work, and then transfer to the PM the responsibility for delivery of the project. There are mixed views within the industry about the effectiveness of Project

Managers. In some cases this may reflect disappointing performance by individual PMs. But it may also be because the PM has been retained after the contract has run into difficulties, or work has already begun and various procurement route options have thereby been blocked off[33]. A PM who is brought in late for "fire fighting" has to assert influence over a contract which may already have gone wrong, and where trust has broken down.

6.14 There is increasing (if sometimes reluctant) acceptance that Project Management, and a separate discipline of Project Managers, are permanent and growing features of the construction scene. But it is probably most satisfactory if the discipline can be provided "in house". The PM will then clearly have the authority of the client to make decisions. If it is necessary to retain an external consultant as PM, the client should first decide whether such an additional level of fees will be justified by the value of the project, or whether a lead designer[34] can also act in that capacity. Where external expertise is required (and justified), one very effective approach might be for an individual to be identified with the necessary skills and seconded into the client's organisation. This should ensure that the PM not only has the requisite expertise but also has authority to act on the client's behalf and has undivided loyalties.[35] Where a design and construct route is chosen, the client's representative/employer's agent should not be there to manage the project - which is the job of the contractor, to whom that risk has been allocated - but to represent the interest of the client if problems arise. "Project Manager" is an inappropriate and confusing term for the client's representative in design and construct procurement.

6.15 There is also a feeling that Project Management requires more training and a clearer status in the industry. The Association of Project Managers (APM) is growing, and gave helpful evidence to the Review. The Chartered Institute of Building published in 1992 a Code of Practice for Project Management for construction and development, which sets out a job specification for a PM, and guidance on the PM's role within the process. Considerable work is in progress to formulate a Level 5 National Vocational Qualification (NVQ) for Project Management, as a post graduate qualification. A single, generally agreed list of responsibilities and duties for Project Managers would be desirable. Discussions between the APM, the DOE and the CIC should be held to achieve this.

6.16 Clients, including Government Departments, should not automatically go down the route of appointing an external Project Manager in a separate role. For some projects they might do better to transfer risk to the contractor under the design and construct route or to use a lead manager responsible for the co-ordination of other consultants, who also undertakes design or supervision. Nor is there any clear benefit from Government Departments having their own procurement systems or requiring external Project Managers to devise their own prequalification arrangements. But whatever the procurement route chosen, there should always be provision for separate adjudication.

6.17 Some criticism was expressed to the Review, particularly in Scotland, about the experience and training of some Departmental project **sponsors**. While it is important that they should be able to call upon expert advice at pre-contract strategy stage from an independent professional, and later from a client's representative, lead or Project Manager, training courses for sponsors within the Civil Service should be fully discussed with construction experts, including clients.

---

[33] *See, e.g., NAO report "Relocation of the Patent Office", February 1994, paragraph 3.14. "By the time the consultant Project Director was appointed in November 1988, the fast track contract strategy had been agreed, the final sketch design, which formed the basis for tendering on the contract, had been approved and tendering action had begun." See also the description by Mr David Pearce, Construction Project Manager of the year 1992 in "Project" - The Bulletin of the Association of Project Managers - July 1993. He describes how, when he took over a particular site as Project Manager in April 1990, "Bulk Excavation ... was 90% complete, with the concrete frame approximately 20% complete".*

[34] *Who may not necessarily be an architect, as the RIBA themselves accept (evidence, P.9).*

[35] *This approach has been strongly advocated by Mr Peter Rogers of Stanhope.*

6.18 I therefore recommend that:

1. Departmental project sponsors should have sufficient expertise to fulfil their role effectively. Their training should be reviewed, in conjunction with appropriate industry and private client experts, to ensure that it gives them full and practical guidance on the workings of the industry.

2. Before deciding upon their contract strategy, clients should assess if they need a separate Project Manager as well as an internal project sponsor, or whether another procurement route should be followed such as design and construct or the use of a lead manager who also acts in a design and/or supervisory role. There must be a separate adjudicator.

3. If a separate Project Manager is necessary, it should first be considered whether the expertise is available "in house" or whether someone with the necessary expertise might be seconded into the client's organisation.

4. If it is decided to retain an external Project Manager:

   a. The terms of appointment and duties should be clearly defined. A list of duties for Project Managers should be devised.

   b. Clear evidence should be available that the applicants have the necessary practical experience of the industry and specific management skills to carry out their duties on behalf of the client.

   c. Once appointed, the PM should be given necessary authority to ensure the work is carried satisfactorily through to completion.

   d. It is not necessary for the PM to be responsible for selecting and employing the other professional consultants. But if given that role, the PM should be required to follow the quality/price route recommended in the CSCP. The PM's fee bid must also allow for proper remuneration of those other consultants. Clients should seek written assurances from consultants who have been retained by a PM that the fee for which they have been retained is sufficient for them to give a full service in accordance with the terms of their appointment.

   e. Whether or not the PM has been responsible for the selection of the other consultants and/or for their employment, all terms of engagements for consultants should be fully interlocked with each other and the main contract.

   f. Appointment documents for all consultants should contain details of the duties of the retained consultants, specific time scales in which those duties are to be performed, and an arrangement that they should "sign off" their work as properly completed at appropriate stages.

   g. PMs employed by public sector clients should not be required to prepare their own prequalification documents for prospective tenderers. They should draw upon firms which are qualified under the DOE's Contractor Management Information System (CMIS) or ConReg procedures, and invite tenders, following EU requirements where necessary.

Many of these recommendations should also be covered by the CSCP.

6.19 Prequalification is an effective system which allows clients to seek tenders from contractors (and also consultants) of equivalent size, capability and experience. Strictly speaking, this is a two stage procedure. "Qualification" means a contractor getting on to an approved list at all. "Prequalification" means drawing up a list of firms which are suitable for a particular project. The first stage is the necessary gateway to the second. The DOE's CMIS offers a service to all Government Departments[36]. As of 23 February 1994, there were 7893 contractors on the CMIS list[37]. The CMIS application form sent to contractors is 6 sides of A4 paper long, and contains 24 questions. The Department of Transport also maintains a list of contractors. There are about 400 firms on that list, of whom around 40 are capable of undertaking work with the value of over £4 million. The DOT form is six sides of A4 paper and contains 18 questions. Both the DOE and the DOT also ask applicants to submit similar documentation such as company (and parent company) accounts. Most local authorities and other public sector clients also keep lists.

6.20 Such duplication of effort is a wasteful burden for the construction industry. It also adds to clients' costs, not only because of increased prices from firms but also because of the resource implications of maintaining separate lists. Attempts to rationalise the procedures in the past have not met with success. The National Joint Consultative Committee for Building drafted two questionnaires in 1988. The first was a fourteen page A4 document for the inclusion of a contractor in a general approved local authority list. The other was twelve pages, and intended for specific projects. They were unable to reach agreement with the Local Authority Associations upon these proposed forms. The NJCC have now devised two more questionnaires, 14 and 11 pages respectively, for General Lists and Specific Projects. They were due for publication in June 1994. The Northern Ireland Housing Executive (NIHE), which is the largest Government client in Northern Ireland, keeps a "Register of Approved Contractors". It has a nine page form, with 27 questions, accompanied by a nine page guidance note written in clear and simple English, which describes its contracts policy. Both main contractors and subcontractors are required to be registered if they wish to be considered for any NIHE work[38]. There are currently 1200 firms on the NIHE list, and there is a three page, 12 question annual review and reassessment form for those firms already on the list.

6.21 The European Union is taking an increasing interest in qualification systems. CEN, the European Standardisation Body, has been asked to consider the feasibility of drawing up common criteria. The most likely outcome is that a firm which has qualified in its own country within the EU would be permitted to tender for work elsewhere without having also to qualify in the country where it wishes to tender. The lack of a single, central UK system of qualification could effectively deny UK contractors opportunities in the rest of Europe once mutual recognition of EU systems is achieved. This is not a theoretical issue. British firms are already working in other EU countries, and vice versa, but all go through a fresh qualification procedure. Pressure for mutual recognition is likely to be strong, as also are possible harmonisation arrangements for the accreditation of individual skills.

---

[36] *The CMIS list can also be consulted by private clients, in that they would be informed, if they enquire of the DOE, if a specific contractor is on the list.*

[37] *For reference see footnote 28.*

[38] *Electrical contractors are specifically required to be registered with the National Inspection Council for Electrical Installation Contracting, and to have attained quality assurance (QA) certification to at least BS 5750 part 3.*

6.22 It is now appropriate for the DOE to develop CMIS as the central United Kingdom resource. That would provide the basis for an official register of contractors, and subcontractors, and would also assist clients and designers to assess competence under the CDM regulations (see Chapter 7, paragraphs 7.6 to 7.9).

6.23 A registration system for public sector work would allow for other factors to be taken into account in assessing the quality, competence and suitability for work of contractors and subcontractors on the list. Additional questions should also be posed, designed to improve productivity and competitiveness, and relating to quality controls, research and development, training arrangements and specialist skills. I am advised that EU legislation may preclude some of these issues being used as part of the selection process. If this is the case, the Government should consider arguing for amendments to the EU legislation. The Local Government Act 1988 may also require amendment in this regard. The DOE may also wish to include the questions normally asked by local authorities regarding outlawing of discrimination.

Recommendations 15.1 - 15.7: Main Contractors' and Subcontractors' List

6.24 I therefore recommend:

1. As a first step, and as a matter of urgency, the DOE should set up a task force drawn from the public sector as a whole to prepare a single qualification document for contractors seeking to do work for any public sector body. This will need to take account of any special interests particular public bodies may have. The system of public sector Project Managers devising their own prequalification forms should cease.

2. The forms should be issued and received by DOE, who will maintain the list (based on CMIS). CMIS must be consulted before any Government Department or Agency commissions any construction related works, and only approved firms used.

3. CMIS will provide all information on local requirements, and locally based firms. There will therefore be no need for local authorities, housing associations, "free standing" educational establishments, or NHS trusts or health authorities to maintain their own lists, or have separate forms. They should instead use CMIS, which is ideally placed to form the core of a national prequalification system.

4. Once set up, the national system should be developed beyond a "size of project" notation system to a quality register of approved contractors seeking public sector work, with a "Star" system related to performance.

5. A charge should be levied on firms joining the register to help defray the cost to public funds.

6. If compulsory "BUILD" insurance is introduced (see Chapter 11), the insurance companies will wish to be involved in quality inspection/supervision of CMIS contractors. But the whole industry should be concerned with quality issues.

7. Subcontractors hoping for work on public contracts should also be registered, and main contractors should be required as a condition of contract to employ only registered subcontractor firms on public sector work. It may be appropriate to consider a cut-off point for registration of very small firms, provided the main contractor takes full responsibility for their work.

6.25 The length of tender lists has been a contentious matter for decades. The public interest must be defended through real competition. But the costs of tendering (to clients and industry) must also be kept to a sensible level. The Banwell Report, which in turn followed the Simon Committee, made selective tendering a key recommendation. The NJCC's Code of Procedure for Single Stage Selective Tendering recommends that a maximum of six firms should be invited, with 2 names "in reserve" in case some of the initial six decline to tender. The Code of Procedure for 2 Stage Selective Tendering, intended for large or complex schemes, also recommends a maximum of six firms, or four if specialist engineering contractors are involved. Again, two "reserve" names are recommended.

6.26 Most public sector clients are governed by the European Union Works and Services Directives in respect of contracts which exceed a certain value. Mandatory procedures include advertising in the Official Journal. There is a need for clear guidance for public sector clients over exactly what is permitted under EU legislation[39]. Evidence has been given to the Review which shows different interpretations by public sector clients of the EU requirements.

6.27 Many local authorities observe good procurement procedures. Birmingham City Council reported that it had conducted a survey in March of 35 local authorities, of which 21 responded, involving "A mix of Metropolitan Districts, London Boroughs and Shire Counties". 90% said that they comply with the NJCC Codes of Procedure and 100% follow the procurement procedures in the Local Government Act 1988 and the EU directives. (Letter to the CIPS assessor from Birmingham City Council, 30 March 1994.) Unfortunately, not every public client is so wedded to the NJCC Code. For example:

1. A London Borough, in January 1991, received 28 tenders for the installation of heating in occupied flats. The value of the tenders ranged from £129,500 to £228,500.

2. Another London Borough, in December 1993, invited tenders for a school building project through the EU Official Journal, specifying "restricted procedure". They still, partly through a mistake in the wording of the advertisement but also through apparent misunderstanding of the legislation, invited 38 firms to go "on the short list".

3. Some Northern Ireland Departments have open tendering arrangements for work up to half a million pounds in value. While numbers of tenders received by those Departments are not normally excessive, averaging 7 or 8, one sometimes receives up to 30. (Source: N.I. Department of the Environment, April 1994.)

4. The CIEC final report states, that it is "not uncommon for 15 or 20 companies to be invited to price a single contract".

5. Concern over long tender lists was also indicated in two surveys recently carried out by "Contract Journal" (see "Contract Journal", 5 May 1994) and by the SECG (Tendering Survey, May 1994).

---

[39] *Such guidance is currently being prepared by PSP, HM Treasury.*

6.28   The perception of the industry has certainly been that tender lists have increased in recent years, and that most lists are excessive. Tables 7 to 9 show the findings of the "New Builder"/JT Design Build construction industry survey (March 1994) on this matter. It is interesting that a significant proportion of clients are concerned. 36% of clients agreed that lists have grown, 30% believe that the majority of all projects involve excessive lists and 46% think that public sector lists are more likely to be excessive than those in the private sector. (Of the 33 clients polled, 10 were themselves public sector clients.)

TABLE 7: THE NUMBER OF FIRMS BEING INVITED TO TENDER FOR INDIVIDUAL CONTRACTS OVER THE LAST 3 YEARS HAS:

	All Respondents	Material Producers	Constructors	House-builders	Consultants	Clients
Increased significantly	41%	40%	47%	40%	46%	24%
Increased slightly	31%	34%	43%	20%	38%	12%
About the same	19%	16%	8%	20%	15%	42%
Decreased slightly	9%	10%	2%	20%	-%	22%

Source: New Builder/JT Construction Industry Attitude Survey, March 1994.

TABLE 8: THE MAJORITY OF ALL CONSTRUCTION PROJECTS INVOLVE EXCESSIVE TENDER LISTS

	All Respondents	Material Producers	Constructors	House-builders	Consultants	Clients
Strongly Agree	25%	40%	25%	24%	25%	12%
Slightly Agree	33%	32%	33%	38%	42%	18%
Neither	18%	8%	32%	18%	8%	24%
Slightly Disagree	15%	12%	8%	14%	14%	29%
Strongly Disagree	9%	8%	2%	6%	11%	17%

Source: New Builder/JT Construction Industry Attitude Survey, March 1994.

	All Respondents	Material Producers	Constructors	House-builders	Consultants	Clients
Strongly Agree	27%	40%	32%	24%	23%	20%
Slightly Agree	18%	24%	14%	12%	16%	26%
Neither	36%	32%	29%	46%	46%	26%
Slightly Disagree	13%	4%	20%	11%	11%	18%
Strongly Disagree	5%	-%	5%	7%	4%	10%

Source: New Builder/JT Construction Industry Attitude Survey, March 1994.

Design and Construct

6.29 Whilst a sensible list of tenderers is important for traditional procurement routes, it is vital for design and construct work, the cost of which is particularly high. An analysis of the cost of tendering prepared for the Review by 3 national contractors, contrasts and compares the cost of tendering under single stage design and build, traditional procurement and the first stage of a two stage design and build procurement route (see table 10). It will be seen that the single stage design and build costs between nearly twice and 2½ times the cost of stage one under a two stage system, and an even higher percentage compared with traditional procurement routes.

TABLE 10: AN ANALYSIS OF THE COST OF TENDERING

	£5M			£10M			£15M			£25M			£40M			£60M			£80M		
	D&B	Trad	D&B Stage 1 Costs	D&B	Trad	D&B Stage 1 Costs	D&B	Trad	D&B Stage 1 Costs	D&B	Trad	D&B Stage 1 Costs	D&B	Trad	D&B Stage 1 Costs	D&B	Trad	D&B Stage 1 Costs	D&B	Trad	D&B Stage 1 Costs
Design fees	Nil	Nil	Nil	3,000	Nil	Nil	6,000	Nil	Nil	9,000	Nil	3,000	12,000	Nil	5,000	15,000	Nil	6,000	20,000	Nil	7,000
Presentation brochures	2,500	Nil	2,000	3,500	Nil	3,000	5,000	1,500	3,500	6,500	1,500	4,500	10,000	1,500	6,000	10,000	1,500	7,500	10,000	1,500	8,000
Quantities	4,000	Nil	Nil	7,000	Nil	Nil	10,000	Nil	Nil	15,000	Nil	Nil	20,000	Nil	Nil	25,000	Nil	Nil	30,000	Nil	Nil
Enquiries	3,500	3,000	2,500	5,000	4,000	4,000	5,000	5,000	5,000	7,000	6,000	5,000	8,000	7,000	6,000	10,000	8,500	7,000	12,000	10,000	8,000
Estimating	5,000	4,000	3,000	6,000	4,000	4,000	9,000	7,500	5,000	12,000	9,500	6,000	15,000	12,000	7,500	20,000	15,000	9,000	25,000	20,000	10,000
Tender planning	4,000	4,000	2,500	4,000	4,500	3,000	5,000	5,000	3,500	6,000	5,500	4,000	8,000	7,000	5,000	12,000	9,000	6,000	15,000	10,000	6,500
Legal, insure commercial	2,000	2,000	1,000	3,000	3,000	2,000	3,500	3,500	2,500	4,000	4,000	3,000	5,500	5,500	4,000	7,000	7,000	4,500	8,000	8,000	5,000
D&B management	4,000	Nil	3,000	4,000	Nil	3,000	5,000	Nil	4,000	6,000	Nil	4,500	7,500	Nil	6,000	8,500	Nil	7,500	10,000	Nil	7,500
Total	25,000	13,000	14,000	36,000	16,500	19,000	49,500	22,500	23,500	65,500	26,500	30,000	86,000	33,000	39,500	107,500	41,000	47,500	130,000	49,500	52,000
Factor			1.79			1.89			2.11			2.18			2.18			2.26			2.50
Tender value %	0.50	0.26	0.28	0.36	0.17	0.19	0.33	0.15	0.16	0.26	0.11	0.12	0.22	0.08	0.10	0.18	0.07	0.08	0.16	0.06	0.07

Source: CIEC, February 1994.

6.30   In those circumstances, clients ought to limit design and build tenders to 3, with 2 "reserve" names available[40] if someone declines to tender. If a two stage tender system is contemplated, five firms could be invited for the first stage, with either one or two firms going through to the second stage. The two stage path is to be preferred. It is less wasteful of resources. Initial stage one bids would typically involve a conceptual sketch, a brief schedule of rates, a quote for preliminaries with mark up and a method statement[41]. The one (or two) successful firms then go through to the second stage to provide full details and costing of their proposals. I have been advised that two stage tendering can be used by public sector clients under the EU's negotiated procedure where that procedure can be justified. But it would be more difficult to use under the restricted procedure and would depend on tenderers dropping out if they perceived they had little chance of winning the contract (source: HM Treasury, May 1994). There is a strong case for revision of the EU rules to make it easier for public sector clients to adopt responsible, two stage tendering procedures. Departments involved in negotiation within the EU should press for such changes.

6.31   The design and construct route is particularly new in civil engineering. The Department of Transport set up its new Highways Agency on 1 April 1994. The Agency is now "responsible for managing and maintaining the existing motorway and trunk road network in England and for delivering the Government's road programme"[42]. The DOT has introduced its own design and construct contract. The previous intention was that one third of new contracts would be on a design and construct basis by 1996, though that now looks unlikely because of public sector spending constraints. Four such schemes have already been let, of which two have been completed. The principal reason for adopting this procurement route was to transfer the ground investigation risk to contractors. That followed NAO/PAC criticism of the 28% excess of out turn over tender price under the ICE 5th Conditions route, based on the client accepting the ground investigation risk, and subsequent claims valued on a remeasurement basis[43]. The first two design and construct schemes were relatively straightforward projects. One came in under tender price. The other showed an excess, but that was due to a late major variation - the construction of an additional bridge. Other significant steps in civil engineering have included:

1. The success of the Alternative Tendering Initiative by the Scottish Office Roads Directorate, launched in 1991. For major schemes, the options offered to tenderers ranged from an ordinary conventional remeasurement contract under ICE 5th Conditions to the contractor redesigning the whole of the works and delivering the project for a fixed price lump sum and own (shorter) timescale. The initial response from contractors was suspicion, but the subsequent reaction was extremely constructive and as the initiative is being developed, out turn indications satisfactory. On certain projects where full design and construct procedures were used firms have been permitted to pool the cost of assessing ground investigation risk. In one earlier contract (1986) payments for design costs were made to unsuccessful tenderers.

---

[40] *I am advised that for those projects which fall within the scope of EU legislation, "reserve" names may not be used if the "restricted procedure" has been chosen (source: HM Treasury, May 1994).*

[41] *Unfortunately, as stated in the Interim Report, contractors' design and build tenders frequently involve architects providing sketches on a "no win, no fee" basis. Clients should require assurances from design and build tenderers that their own consultants have been and/or will be retained on the same basis of quality and price as if they were being retained directly by the client.*

[42] *Written Answer by the Rt. Hon. John MacGregor, MP, 28 March 1994, Hansard columns 484-5.*

[43] *NAO report "Department of Transport: Contracting for Roads" November 1992, and 43rd report of the Committee of Public Accounts, session 1992/3, "Contracting for Roads", May 1993.*

2. The Lagan Bridge Contract in Belfast involved six firms being selected for the first stage of the tendering process, and three groups of contractors in joint ventures in stage two. The competition made provision for compensation to paid to each of the two unsuccessful tenderers. Consultants assisted the Department, and also Northern Ireland Railways, to assess the technical capability of the outline schemes. The Royal Fine Art Commission gave aesthetic advice on the design proposals.

Recommendations 16.1 - 16.3: Tendering

6.32 I recommend:

1. Detailed advice should be included in the CSCP to all public sector clients on the specific requirements for selective tendering of European Union Directives.

2. Clients should adhere to the recommended numbers of tenders for single stage tendering in the NJCC Code of Procedure. As a general rule, clients subject to EU legislation should not use open tendering procedures. Those Northern Ireland Departments which are currently using open tendering should change to selective tendering procedures unless there are over riding local reasons - in which case they should be stated by Ministers.

3. Clients which seek tenders on a design and build or design and construct basis should proceed by the following tender route:-

    a. Not more than three firms, with one other name in "reserve"[44], should be invited to tender on a single stage basis. This system is best used for simpler contracts with relatively straight forward design input, or where it is intended that a significant proportion of the outline design will be undertaken by the client's own retained consultants before tenders are sought.

    b. A two stage tender procedure should be used for more complex and substantial projects, subject to guidance to public sector clients on EU requirements under the CSCP. A maximum of five firms (with one "reserve") should be approached to tender for the first stage, narrowing the choice down to two (or one, if preferred) for the second stage.

    c. Where substantial ground investigation costs will be incurred by tenderers, they should be permitted to "pool" such costs by retaining a single firm of consultants to act on behalf of them all.

    d. Where very large and expensive schemes are to be carried out, a reasonable proportion of expenses should be paid to unsuccessful tenderers, and this should be made known in advance.

    e. Assurances should be sought from contractors that their own professional consultants have been and/or will be retained on a quality and price basis.

---

[44] *The "reserve" system may not be used for projects tendered under the EU's restricted procedure.*

6.33   The Interim Report stressed that clients should choose their contractors (and consultants) on a value for money basis, with proper weighting of criteria for skill. Choice of the lowest tender may neglect considerations of cost in use or indeed final (out turn) cost of the project. The Association of Metropolitan Authorities commented "as a matter of public accountability and, in some cases, legal requirement, local authorities are at present compelled to accept the lowest valid tender." (Letter to CIPS Assessor, April 1994.)

6.34   This concern was echoed by a senior official of a particular local authority:

"Local authorities are severely hampered by being forced to accept the lowest tender. I know that we are not so forced but the overpowering attitude of local authority officers is that for all intents and purposes we are ... I could envisage a quite dramatic reversal of the adversarial attitudes if local authorities, or any other employer group for that matter, chose the tenderer who quoted closest to the "average" price as a matter of principle and let the tenderers know that from the outset. It might cost the employers some money "up-front" but would allow for more accurate budgeting and forecasting than is currently the case". (Source: Letter from Mr John Lane, External Client Manager, Brighton Borough Council April 1994.)

6.35   The National Audit Office have made it plain that it is not necessary to choose the lowest tender. The **best** tender should be accepted. The NAO expect clear evidence that a public authority has been through a considered route of evaluating tenders if the lowest is not to be chosen. Some evidence to the Review has suggested that the lowest and highest tenders should **automatically** be discarded. I do not agree. One of those tenders might be the best one. Some public authorities see the danger of choosing a tender which is too low to generate any profit for the contractor. Leicestershire County Council has recently introduced a procedure for evaluating the performance of contractors. The Director of Property writes:

"The objective of this procedure is to provide a structured and equitable means of assessing each contractor's performance, against set criteria, which will include workmanship, site supervision, cost control, adherence to programme, contract administration etc. Evaluation results will influence the selection process for future contracts and poor performance could lead to contractors being considered for removal from the County Council's standing list...

"Whilst the Department of Property continues to procure construction work for its clients on a "most cost advantageous" basis, because there have a limited number of instances where abnormally low tenders have been matched by substandard performance, it is intended that the evaluation procedure will facilitate a sensible "value for money" basis for future contracts, where cost and quality are the key factors.

"Initially, to assist in setting up a computer database, the performance of contractors on all contracts achieving practical completion in the last twelve months will be evaluated. The procedure will then be implemented for every current and future contract." (Source: Letter to contractors from Mr P A C Smith, Director of Property, Leicestershire County Council, 14 March 1994.)

6.36   That robust approach should be welcomed. Best procedures should be the norm. I have already made recommendations regarding selection/qualification procedures. They will take some time to introduce. Meanwhile, the DOE should include in the CSCP a recommendation that public authorities, including local authorities, should seek to evaluate all tenders on the basis of quality, likely cost-in-use and out turn price and known past performance, as well as price. It should also state that auditors will be prepared to accept that price should not be the only criterion, provided that a clear audit trail is established by which quality is assessed. A clear statement of Government policy along those lines will, by itself, be of significant assistance and comfort to public clients[45].

6.37   It may be argued that if a responsible qualification system has previously been gone through, there is no need for further scrutiny of tenders. Indeed, the NJCC Code for Selective Tendering says so. "The object of selection is to make a list of firms, any one of which could be entrusted with the job. If this is achieved, then the final choice of contractor will be simple - the firm offering the lowest tender. Only the most exceptional cases justify departure from this general recommendation." Unfortunately, clients also need to protect themselves against apparently responsible qualified firms which are prepared to "buy" work at an uneconomic tender price simply in order to generate cash flow. When contracts are won on a price which can only produce a loss for the main contractor, the likelihood of a contract dominated by claims, and of disputes between main contractor and subcontractors, is extremely high. Clients, with their professional advisers, need to be able to reject an apparently financially advantageous tender because it is uneconomic. Alternatively, a higher tender may offer a client a new approach or save on the whole life cost of the project. In drawing up criteria for such decisions, the advice by the CUP relating to competitive fees for consultants is equally appropriate regarding contractors. "A loss making contract is normally a recipe for trouble"[46]. The criteria used for evaluation should be included in the tender documents. For contracts subject to EU requirements, this is already a requirement.[47] Uneconomic tenders subject to EU directives cannot be rejected out of hand. Tenderers must be allowed to seek to justify them.

6.38   Preparation of tenders should not be hurried. The NJCC Codes of Procedure set out clear and specific time scales to be allowed for the submission of tenders, and these should be followed. If the main contractors are rushed to prepare their documents, it is inevitable that pressure will be placed upon the subcontractors as well. Other aspects of good practice contained in the NJCC Code such as opening of bids, notifying all tenderers of the outcome and post-tender project planning should also be adhered to as a matter of course by clients. A hasty project is unlikely to proceed smoothly. Everyone will lose, and the client most of all.

---

[45] *I understand that in CCT Guidance to local authorities which is due to be published in June on the "Avoidance of Anti-Competitive Behaviour", the Government makes clear that it is for local authorities to decide on the appropriate balance between price and quality and to select the appropriate tender accordingly.*

[46] *CUP Guidance Note 13.*

[47] *See CUP Guidance Note 26B paragraph 5.2.*

6.39 The aim should be for the DOE to set up a central qualification list based on CMIS of contractors and subcontractors seeking public sector work. Such a list should also be supported by a national scheme of guidance for quality assessment of tenders. But pending its introduction:

1. The DOE should remind all public authorities through the CSCP that those tenders which offer the best value for money ("economically advantageous" in EU terminology) and show clear regard for cost-in-use should be accepted.

2. Public authorities should publish their own criteria for quality assessment in their tender documents, prior to the establishment of a national scheme.

3. The CSCP should remind clients that it is desirable to adhere to proposals in the NJCC Codes of Procedures relating to timescales for submission of tenders, opening of bids, notification of tenderers and post-tender project planning.

Selection of Subcontractors

6.40 The benefits of an orderly and fair selection procedure, of short, but competitive tender lists and of consideration of quality as well as price apply to the selection of subcontractors by main contractors (and further down the chain), as well as to the selection of contractors by clients. Many of my recommendations should have a beneficial, knock-on effect to this selection process. However, further specific action is required.

6.41   I recommend that the CIEC and the Constructors Liaison Group (CLG) should produce a joint Code of Practice for the Selection of Subcontractors (by main contractors and by other subcontractors). This should contain:

1.   Commitments to short tender lists (especially for design and construct work).

2.   Commitments to selection on quality and price (especially for work with a design input).

3.   The contractor should confirm, when offering a subcontract document to domestic subcontractors, that it complies with the principles set out in Chapter 5 of this Report and with the provisions of the Construction Contracts Bill (see Chapter 8). A similar procedure should be adopted by first line subcontractors to their sub-subcontractors. (Below that level this should only be followed if formal contract documentation is used.) A similar system is used on public sector schemes in Germany.

4.   Dutch auctioning should be explicitly ruled out. Specific provision should be made for tenders to be opened simultaneously at a predetermined time, date and place, and in the presence of the tenderers or their nominees, or of a mutually acceptable independent witness.[48]

5.   Main contractors should notify clients automatically in advance of the commencement of work of the names and addresses of all firms of domestic subcontractors to be employed on the site, whether or not they have previously "named" them, so that they can exercise the right to object to any. This should relate only to the first level of subcontractors.

6.   Subcontractors should undertake that, in the spirit of teamwork, they will co-ordinate their activities effectively with each other, and thereby assist the achievement of the main contractor's overall programme. They may need to price for such interface work. (This is part of the "win-win" culture in the USA and Germany.)

Public clients should require adherence to the Code by firms tendering for public sector work. Other client organisations should strongly encourage their members to do likewise.

Partnering

6.42   The Banwell Report indicated that there was scope for awarding contracts in certain circumstances without competition to contractors who had shown particularly good performance on behalf of clients. Such "serial contracting" or "negotiation" is especially suitable where it represents a follow on stage to a previous contract, either on an adjoining site or as a logical sequence to it. Public sector clients will need to follow EU procedures, where appropriate.

---

[48] *The Canadian bid depository system offers a possible model for implementation. In Québec, all tenders apparently pass through this system. (Source: SECG/Mechanical Contractors Association of Canada, March 1994.)*

6.43 It is possible to go further, and for client and contractor to enter into a specific and formal partnering agreement. This is a contractual arrangement between the two parties for either a specific length of time or for an indefinite period. The parties agree to work together, in a relationship of trust, to achieve specific primary objectives by maximising the effectiveness of each participant's resources and expertise. It is not limited to a particular project.

6.44 Such a system can be very effective in large programmes where it is desirable to build up expert teams and keep them together. Process plant and power station construction are particularly suitable, but there could be the use of such relationships in building as well. The DOE may wish to indicate to other public sector clients that such relationships could be beneficial and certainly deserve some experiments. The partner should initially be sought through a competitive process, which would be necessary to meet EU requirements.[49]

6.45 As a client organisation (some of whose members are instinctively wary of partnering in case it produces "cosy" relationships), the CIPS acknowledges in its final report that partnering has a place in procurement. "Partnering includes the concepts of teamwork between supplier and client, and of total continuous improvement. It requires openness between the parties, ready acceptance of new ideas, trust and perceived mutual benefit. Partnering can only be successful with the commitment of the Chief Executives of the organisations involved, and by the selection of individuals with a determination to work together. We are confident that partnering can bring significant benefits by improving quality and timeliness of completion whilst reducing costs. It can be applied to the construction industries through longer term agreements or option contracts."

6.46 Partnering arrangements are also beneficial between firms. Some main contractors have developed long term relationships with subcontractors. That is welcome. Such arrangements should have the principal objective of improving performance and reducing costs for clients. They should not become "cosy". The construction process exists to satisfy the client. Good relationships based on mutual trust benefit clients.

Recommendation 19: Partnering

6.47 Specific advice should be given to public authorities so that they can experiment with partnering arrangements where appropriate long-term relationships can be built up[50]. But the partner must initially be sought through a competitive tendering process, and for a specific period of time. Any partnering arrangement should include mutually agreed and measurable targets for productivity improvements.

---

[49] *Further details of partnering are available in "Partnering: Contracting without Conflict" published by NEDC, 1991, and "In Search of Partnering Excellence" published by the United States Construction Industry Institute, July 1991. See also paragraph 15.5 of the White Paper "Competitiveness - Helping Business to Win", HMSO, May 1994.*

[50] *This advice might build on existing Treasury guidance "Partnering in the Public Sector", July 1993.*

7.1   Unequivocal evidence about performance on site, and how the British construction industry compares with other countries, is hard to find. Some surveys have been carried out, which may show that British performance is below that of some of our international competitors. Some large clients certainly believe this to be so, and have taken steps to introduce new techniques, systems of procurement and research to raise the standards of British construction. For example:

1.   Lynton plc found that the cost of producing a typical US office building in North Carolina to be 32% lower than a similar building at Heathrow. The divergence arose from differences in specification levels and greater use of standard components in the USA. (Source: "The UK Construction Challenge", 1993.)

2.   Stanhope reported that during the period 1985 to 1991 they regularly achieved construction savings of around 30% compared to industry norms. They are looking for further significant reductions, setting specific targets and involved in benchmarking research in the USA and Japan. They are currently studying possible over-specification of floor loadings and mechanical and electrical systems. They are also looking to extensive use of prefabrication and modulisation to improve on-site efficiency. (Source: "Setting Standards in the Construction Industry", October 1993.)

3.   McDonald's Restaurants Ltd has used a great deal of off-site prefabrication for its fast food outlets. It has reduced cost and time of construction in the UK over the last five years by 60%, and on-site construction times from 115 to 15 days. It uses modular techniques and treats production as an engineering exercise. It is looking for further improvements, including standardisation of foundations. It agrees on a yearly programme with producers so as to build up familiarity, team work and performance (source: McDonald's Restaurants Ltd).

7.2   "Strategies for the European Construction Sector - A Programme for Change", the report prepared by W S Atkins for the European Commission, found the United Kingdom to have high construction costs compared to other EU countries but almost the lowest wage costs. Japan, after calculation of purchasing power parity (PPP) to minimise differences in exchange rates, is shown to have the lowest cost for building compared with the EC and USA. These findings are set out in tables 11 and 12. Some of the differences may be accounted for by different levels of specifications.

TABLE 11: CONSTRUCTION COST INDICATORS, 1990

(UK = 100; rounded estimates)

	Buildings		Public Works		Total at PPP
	Market Rate	at PPP	Market Rate	at PPP	
UK	100	100	100	100	200
Netherlands	105	105	87	86	191
Italy	84	97	79	92	189
Denmark	117	107	79	72	181
Spain	73	94	65	84	178
Ireland	82	96	70	81	177
Greece	70	100	53	76	176
Belgium	82	96	68	79	175
Germany	97	96	75	74	170
France	81	101	54	67	168
Portugal	53	98	34	63	161
EC Median	82	98	75	79	177
Turkey	35	na	20	na	na
Japan	86	77	98	88	165
USA	73	108	76	112	220

Source: W S Atkins from OECD data, Table 5.1 of "Strategies for the European Construction Industry - A Programme for Change" prepared by W S Atkins for the European Commission, published by the European Commission, May 1994.

TABLE 12: RELATIONSHIP BETWEEN PROJECT COSTS AND LABOUR COSTS, EC COUNTRIES

Cost index (UK=100) at PPP

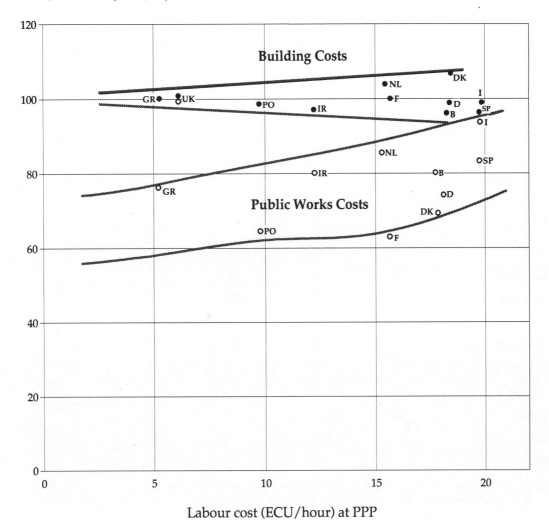

Labour cost (ECU/hour) at PPP

*Source: Figure 5.4, from"Strategies for the European Construction Industry - A Programme for Change"
prepared by W S Atkins for the European Commission, published by the European Commission,
May 1994.*

7.3   Some performance issues can be, and are being, addressed through new procurement
routes or new technology, such as Knowledge Based Engineering. There is scope for
improvements through greater standardisation of components and design details and
more off-site prefabrication. This will require effective teamwork by designers, contractors,
subcontractors and manufacturers. Specialist engineering contractors believe that better
collaboration in design between consulting engineer and specialist could produce a target
cost saving of 20%.[51] But removing other obstacles to progress involves a new look at
competence, training and education, research and development.

---

[51] *c/f Paper by Mr Martin Davis to the SPIM conference on construction management, 25th March
1994, in which a detailed breakdown of the 20% calculation is given.*

7.4   It is widely agreed within the industry that it is too easy to set up in business as a general contractor. No qualifications are required, no experience and virtually no capital. While market forces ultimately remove incompetent firms by depriving them of work, the existence of such unskilled producers is a threat to responsible firms, bad for consumers and highly damaging to the wider reputation of the industry.

7.5   There are two main ways to address this difficulty. They are registration/accreditation of main contractors (and specialist/trade contractors) and/or accreditation of operatives. A distinction may be drawn between work for public sector clients which is publicly funded, whether as a whole or in part, and that carried out for the private sector. This review is not directly concerned with minor repair or other domestic household work, which is normally carried out without any formal contract document. But if standards can be raised in the industry generally, it might also assist in that sector.[53]

CDM

7.6   A new feature in the debate over quality is the Construction (Design and Management) Regulations 1994 ("CDM"). Subject to transitional provisions, they should come into force on 1 October (though this date has still to be confirmed). They arise in part from the Temporary or Mobile Construction Sites Directive of the European Union. The CDM regulations exclude[54].

1.   Projects that are not expected to employ more than four persons on site at any one time or to last more than 30 working days.

2.   Projects for domestic clients.

3.   Minor works in premises normally inspected by a local authority.

Subject to these exclusions, new statutory duties are placed upon clients, designers and contractors of all kinds. There will be a duty to consider safety and health from the outset of a project, systematically and at each stage. It will be necessary to involve all who can contribute to it. There must be proper planning and co-ordination of safety aspects from the outset, and throughout the project. Health and safety provision must be adequately resourced and carried out by competent persons. Information must be shared and communicated, and must also be recorded for future reference.

---

[52] *Some (especially the CIEC) prefer to avoid the expression "registration" because of its allegedly bureaucratic overtones.*

[53] *Neither is the Review concerned with private house building for sale, where there is de facto compulsory registration and insurance cover.*

[54] *The duties for designers still apply to projects falling under (1) and (2).*

7.7 Under CDM, there are specific duties for:-

1. **Clients**

   They must appoint competent designers and contractors. They will also have to appoint a planning supervisor, a new appointment, though it may be filled by a competent person who is also involved in the project in another capacity (e.g. an architect).

2. **Planning Supervisors**

   They must co-ordinate health and safety considerations by designers, ensure a health and safety plan is prepared, prepare a health and safety file and be in a position to advise clients and contractors on competency and on the adequate provision of resources for a safe working environment.

3. **Designers (of all kinds)**

   They must take specific account of health and safety risks in their design work and take steps to eliminate, reduce or control them and provide relevant information.

4. **Principal Contractors**

   They must create and maintain a health and safety plan and ensure that it is implemented, including by all other contractors or subcontractors.

These statutory duties involve criminal offences if it can be shown that someone failed to take proper steps to ensure competence.

7.8 The CDM regulations may represent a step towards de facto registration of contractors. The Courts will require to be convinced that a client has taken proper steps to appoint competent people. It is likely to be a defence if a client can show that a contractor was appointed who had both experience and previous competence. The proposals in this Report for expanding the scope of CMIS to include all contractors and subcontractors seeking public sector work will in practice be a registration system. The Northern Ireland Housing Executive describes its equivalent of CMIS as an "Approved List". A combination of:

1. the drive for a European system of prequalification;

2. the competence requirements of CDM; and

3. the need for high standards of performance

make the registration of firms under CMIS a potential gateway to public sector work.

7.9   As far as private sector work is concerned, little purpose would be achieved by having a massive central register of thousands of self-employed people. Apart from the immense bureaucracy of keeping it up to date, such people are unlikely to be involved as principals in work under standard contract conditions, and, even if they are, it is likely to be on very small jobs below the CDM threshold. Registration should in any case be voluntary. Firms which wish to have some form of registration, but do not to wish to apply either for CMIS (or to be registered with the National House Building Council) can seek it through responsible industry trade associations. Many associations already have codes of conduct. Some also provide consumer guarantees, warranty schemes or informal arbitration procedures between dissatisfied consumers and member firms. Clients will be able to establish, before asking a firm to tender for work, whether:

1.   that firm, and its proposed subcontractors, are registered with CMIS; or

2.   it is part of a voluntary industry/trade association warranty scheme, or other consumer protection scheme; and/or

3.   it has some other form of recognised quality assurance system in place.

Such arrangements will not of themselves guarantee quality. But they will indicate to a client that the firm has a track record and some serious basis of skill and experience.

Operatives

7.10   The accreditation of operatives is also highly desirable, as a method of raising the skills base of the industry. The success over many years of the scaffolders accreditation system, or of the Institute of Plumbing, show that specific schemes to raise individual standards can be very effective. The industry itself is about to launch such a national system, the Construction Skills Certification Scheme, ultimately to be linked to achieved skill standards under NVQs. This initiative is greatly to be welcomed, and long overdue. It should receive Government endorsement and support.

7.11   Concern has also been expressed to the Review about the wide extent of self-employment in the industry. Inland Revenue statistics for 1992 show that for the year 1989/90 (the latest analyzed) 1.18 million self-employed tax payers were engaged in building and contracting. That number includes contractors or working principals who are not part of the labour only subcontracting system, or working in gangs. It is thought by the Inland Revenue Staff Federation that self-employed subcontractors total about 700,000[55].

7.12   I appreciate and respect this concern. Responsible firms in the industry say that such workers are really employed, but that their self-employed status reduces the overhead costs which they (or their co-ordinators where they work in teams) have to carry. But I do not feel that I can recommend a statutory return to employed status as a general rule. Individuals who wish to work on a self-employed basis should be permitted to do so. However, they must accept the risks which real self-employment involves. Treasury Ministers have already announced proposals intended to improve the effectiveness of the Tax Deduction Scheme, though it will take four years to introduce the new arrangements. If the effect is to bring about a return to directly employed status by those who were never

---

[55] *Source: Correspondence shown to the Review by the Transport and General Workers Union, figures relating to April 1993. The GMB also estimate that "perhaps 60% of the total UK building and civil engineering labour force is allegedly self-employed" (evidence, January 1994).*

really self-employed in the first place, that alone may help to improve training arrangements and closer supervision of performance on site. It may also reduce unfair competition for firms which discharge their statutory responsibilities for paying taxes and other charges.

7.13 Training in the industry is provided mainly under the auspices of the Construction Industry Training Board (CITB), one of only two remaining statutory boards. Certain specialist sections of the industry are not within the scope of the CITB, and have their own training schemes. The SECG, in its final report, made it clear that it had no wish to return to the CITB, claiming that "since withdrawal from CITB, there has been a dramatic increase in training awareness, responsibility and activity". Some sectors of the industry which remain in scope also have doubts.[56] But the general contracting industry itself largely favours the continuation of the Board and a compulsory levy, so as to ensure some degree of sharing of training costs.[57]

7.14 The CITB has responded positively to widespread concern about training and career opportunities in the industry. It has recently published the Report of the Joint Action Group on New Entrant Training (JAGNET), entitled "Proposals for the Construction Industry Training Scheme for Craft and Operative New Entrants" (March 1994). It contains 42 recommendations, and a proposed timescale for their implementation, beginning on 1st April 1995.

7.15 Youth training represents the predominant intake into the industry, with 68% of the first year intake in 1992 being first year YTs (source: JAGNET report, table 10). The sharp fall in traditional apprenticeships in many industries has concerned Ministers, who recently announced a new Government initiative for "modern apprenticeships". Under that initiative, as from September 1995 new style apprenticeships will be offered to 16 and 17 year old school leavers. The arrangements will involve four Training and Enterprise Councils offering prototypes in electrical installation and two in engineering construction[58]. The CITB itself is also taking part, with two separate trial schemes to be launched in Sussex and Manchester in the autumn of 1994[59]. They will be linked to NVQ3 level qualifications.

7.16 The JAGNET report offers detailed proposals for training within construction. In particular, it addresses possible methods of involving labour-only subcontractors more effectively within the training structures, and suggests new grants for that purpose. It contains a comprehensive package for implementation, and should be discussed urgently by the industry and the Government.

---

[56] *The National Association of Shopfitters, whose members are in CITB scope, says that "there is still a strong body of shopfitters who feel that CITB does not cater adequately for the specialist training requirements of the shopfitting industry". (evidence, April 1994). Shopfitting is officially classified as a manufacturing industry, and much of its work is factory based.*

[57] *c/f CIEC final report, paragraph 5.28.*

[58] *Miss A. Widdecombe MP, Hansard, 29 March 1994, column 701, written answers.*

[59] *CITB Press Announcement, 28th April 1994. Regarding "modern apprenticeships" for 16/17 year olds and also the proposed "accelerated modern apprenticeships" for 18/19 year olds, see the White Paper, "Competitiveness - Helping Business to Win" HMSO, May 1994, Chapter 4.*

7.17 In its final report to this Review, the CIEC makes several specific recommendations on training.

1. "Modern apprenticeships" must be flexible enough to be accommodated within the realities of 60% self-employment among the workforce.

2. There should be a national TEC for construction, based on the CITB.

3. NVQs in the industry are not yet fully developed or satisfactory, and arrangements for output-related funding are undermining the system.

4. The CITB levy exclusion threshold should be abolished.

5. CITB must reduce its operating costs and raise to 85% the proportion of its levy income which is distributed in grants.

Recommendation 20: Training

7.18 These substantial proposals on training by the CIEC have not been discussed by me with the Assessors or considered in detail by the Review, through lack of time. However, they should be examined as a matter of urgency by the industry and the Government, in conjunction with the JAGNET report itself.

Other Training Issues

7.19 The Institute of Roofing (IOR), in written and oral evidence to the Review, expressed concern at the level of representation of smaller subcontractors on organisations concerned with training, and particularly on the Construction Industry Standing Conference, which is concerned with the development of National Vocational Qualifications within the construction industry. The Institute favoured the formation of a Council which offered one seat to every specialist and trade contractor organisation. I make no recommendation about the IOR's proposal, which has not been advocated by the NSCC, the SECG or the Building Structures Group in their final reports. The NSCC has recommended that "the National Council for Vocational Qualifications should be far more responsive to industry requirements and react to the needs of industry". It is important that the voice of small firms should be heard on training matters, especially as it is difficult for such business people to find time to serve voluntarily on committees. The Constructors Liaison Group (CLG) should give the specific problem of the representation of smaller firms further consideration.

7.20 Although Ministerial responsibility for the CITB rests with the Department of Employment and education is a matter for the Department for Education, it is important that the Construction Sponsorship Directorate of the DOE is closely involved in discussions about industrial training in the construction industry. The availability of a well trained and efficient workforce is vital for the industry.

7.21   Training is not only a matter of procedures. There is a deeper issue. One of the main problems facing the industry is how to attract a high calibre of young person into construction firms. (There seems to be no problem in recruiting high quality architectural students. Most courses are over subscribed.) The Principal of Glasgow College of Building and Printing commented "with regard to the recruitment of able young persons it is essential that the image of the industry is improved, with particular emphasis placed on schools and parents". (Letter from Principal Thomas Wilson, February 1994.) This is not a difficulty which is restricted to Britain. The EC/WS Atkins report on the EU construction industry found that "construction work is often seen as an unattractive option. It is perceived as dirty, dangerous, exposed to bad weather, unhealthy, insecure, underpaid, of low status and with poor career prospects for educated people."

7.22   The CITB has tried to tackle this problem through its network of over 70 Curriculum Centres. These seek to bring together schools and Colleges of Further Education with the local construction industry. This pre-vocational initiative needs fuller support from employers. If the industry is to be become more attractive to young people (and their families and teachers) it needs better physical conditions on site and improved career prospects.

7.23   The industry should also take direct action to portray itself more favourably, a topic which was of concern to the authors of the "Towards 2001" report[60]. Some action could be quite inexpensive, such as mobile road shows to schools, colleges, agricultural shows, careers conventions, and perhaps some sporting events, which could contain videos and photographic examples of fine completed projects to raise the public profile of the industry. A "visit to sites" initiative - as was undertaken by the Chartered Institute of Building (CIOB) some years ago - could also do much to show the public how the industry really works. If the industry does not display pride in its own considerable achievements it can hardly expect others to enthuse for it. The nature of the industry's business is such that it rarely advertises direct to the public, other than specialist sectors such as private house builders, "Do it Yourself" stores or merchants, or tradespeople seeking domestic work from households through outlets such as Yellow Pages or local newspapers.

7.24   Women are seriously under represented in the industry. There is no obvious reason why this should be so at a professional consultant level, while the traditional excuses offered in respect of site operatives are becoming less relevant as the building process becomes more mechanised, there is more off-site prefabrication and plant replaces labour. In its final report, the CIC states "a major obstacle to the industry's ability to recruit the best people is the fact that half of the population is largely ignored by the industry. At professional level, there are exceptions to this, but as a recent CIC survey showed few of the professional institutions have one woman member for every ten men." CIC conducted a survey of the number of women professionals amongst the membership of 14 of the professional institutions in the construction industry. It showed that in 1992/1993, there were 12,406 women out of a total collective membership of 239,700 across the 14 disciplines, equal to 5.2% of the total.

---

[60] *"Building Towards 2001" report in 1991 by the National Contractors Group of the Building Employers Confederation and the Centre for Strategic Studies in Construction, Reading University.*

7.25 The industry must tackle these problems directly.

1. "Building Towards 2001" made eleven recommendations for improvements. Some of them are also addressed by this Review, such as "Changing the structure within which the industry handles contracts and works with designers". The CIEC and the CLG should set up a high powered task force to report quickly on implementation of "2001's" recommendations for the industry to improve its image, and how to finance such a campaign. Other parts of the industry have already done so. Material producers are extensive individual advertisers and some also engage in collective advertising of products. Private house builders and manufacturers/suppliers have successfully financed collective publicity through the New Homes Marketing Board. If it is agreed to form a Construction Industry Development Agency (see Chapter 12), such marketing could become part of its duties.

2. Equal opportunities must also be vigorously pursued by the industry, with encouragement from Government. The CIC, CIEC and CLG should produce co-ordinated action plans to promote equal opportunities within the industry and to widen the recruitment base.

Professional Education

7.26 The Interim Report asked whether professional education needed a greater content of practical experience. I do not need to make detailed recommendations on this issue, since extensive work, and many proposals, are made in the following reports:-

1. "Crossing Boundaries", by Professor John Andrews and Sir Andrew Derbyshire, published by the CIC, April 1993.

2. "Steering Group on Architectural Education - Report and Recommendations", report of the group chaired by Mr Richard Burton, published by the RIBA, June 1992.

3. "The Strategic Study of the Profession" phase 1, "Strategic Overview", published by the RIBA, May 1992, and phase 2, "Clients & Architects", October 1993.

7.27 Those reports have respectively 3 pages (CIC), 6 pages (Burton Report) and 5 pages (Phase 2 RIBA Survey) of specific recommendations or "Agenda for Change". The CIC provided me with a checklist of their recommendations which had been implemented or were being addressed, and this is at Appendix 5. It is clear from many responses to me by architects themselves that there is a feeling in that great and honoured profession that it should widen the practical content of its educational courses.

1. The Association of Consultant Architects commented:

   "We would agree that the architect, in common with all other professionals, (we include in this definition the contractors) needs special training to meet the needs of an improved understanding. Continuing Professional Development

(CPD), an NVQ 5 for Project Management is on the stocks and the ever enlarging choice of University courses give encouragement to the accomplishment of this objective....

".... The ACA would look for .... modules of education which could be held in common and where individuals in the total industry could meet in their formative years. These might include financial and management skills. The cross course facilities of the modern emerging Universities should be used to provide these facilities and this should be promoted by them as their contribution to industry. More esoteric courses might still exist, and perhaps should exist, because architects, in common with other professionals apply themselves to many fields of endeavour.

"This could be developed in the major business staff colleges with mid-career courses for the leaders of the project team as a whole.

".... The only way we will engender the "right spirit" within the industry is by being more **cohesive** and **better educated**."[61]

2. The RIBA added "We share the general concern for the promotion of management and financial skills, which feature in the professional studies element of the prequalification education and training and in CPD provision, but which merit even greater attention. For many years our Practical Training scheme has provided for site experience appropriate to the nascent architect - it is accepted that actual achievement in this respect is not easy to accomplish and may be less than desirable. It needs constant monitoring and promotion" (evidence, April 1994).

3. The RIAS commented "on-site experience has for architectural students and graduates sadly been limited recently because of the downturn in the building industry. ...There may be merit in enacting a set minimum time [between graduation and] seeking membership of [the RIAS] based on an increase on the current average, with the extra time being employed in site and contract administration experience" (evidence, April 1994).

7.28 It is for the professions to consider, develop and approve the educational courses and qualifications which they deem necessary for entry. But a good deal is going on already. As the ACA rightly points out, Universities are already developing new courses[62]. Some, such as the new part time course at Masters Level at Cambridge University on "Inter Disciplinary Design for the Built Environment" (supported by the Ove Arup Foundation) are intended for graduate professionals already involved with the built environment. The Scottish Schools of Architecture have formed an association which has devised a multi-disciplinary third year design competition known as "Interact" (source: RIAS evidence). There is lively debate on the relationship between NVQs or SVQs at levels 4 & 5 and professional education, and the "competence" criteria which they should involve, which hopefully will be resolved soon.

---

[61] *The ACA are quoting from a letter of Mr Peter Rogers - see paragraph 7.29 (3) (ACA evidence, March 1994).*

[62] *For example, The Faculty of the Built Environment at the University of Central England in Birmingham has developed a "modular built environment degree programme incorporating up to 20% commonality across 6 (or 7, in 1994 - 1995) vocational degree programmes. The common units underpin shared and specialist units within each course. All courses have clearly defined routes to professional qualifications" ("BEEDS" Newsletter of the Faculty, February 1994).*

7.29 In general, there is an acceptance that a greater inter disciplinary approach is necessary, without losing the expertise of individual professions. For example:-

1. "Although there is little doubt that professionals need to understand more clearly the role each other has to play in the building process, it is also important not to lose specialisms that are so important to the industry as it becomes more and more complex. Professional education needs to supplement these specialisms with a thorough grounding in management and financial training for all disciplines." (CIOB evidence, March 1994.)

2. "The educational needs of the built environment could be improved by the introduction of more inter disciplinary work at undergraduate level, to enhance the understanding and awareness of the problems, roles and contributions of construction professionals. However, such improvement must not be at the expense of specific skills and competence of each particular discipline." (International Procurement Review Group[63] evidence, March 1994.)

3. "I believe the only way we will engender the "right spirit" within the industry is by being more cohesive and better educated. I am not a supporter of the "totally integrated" degree course since there are differences between arts and science students which should be built upon, rather than amalgamated in the hope of producing the all rounded "construction" graduate ..... I would try to integrate the disciplines more by having graduates work together, particularly in their later years when they can be of use to each other. For example, setting a project that would involve both architects and engineers working together, in say their second or third years when they had enough knowledge of their particular subjects to be of value to each other." (Letter from Mr Peter Rogers of Stanhope, December 1993.)

4. ".... establish a 2 year course .... leading to a qualification as Construction Architect .... The syllabus would include a thorough grounding in the resources available to the industry: finance, land, labour, materials, technology and co-ordination. In particular, a systematic study of ways in which the client's conceptual requirements can be realised through progressive design stages.... The focus on integrated design could be more effective ... for architects at part 2 level. The normal course in architecture up to part 1 would thus give students the opportunity to specialise in conceptual or constructional design at second degree level. The timing could be broadened by industry sponsorship immediately after "A" Level. Students would then be introduced to the construction process in vacations and possibly during the "year out", prior to embarking on part 2". (Paper by Mr Bryan Jefferson, June 1993.)

---

[63] *The IPRG involves the Departments of Property and Development Studies, University of Glamorgan, the School of Built Environment, Liverpool John Moores University and the Department of Surveying, Nottingham Trent University.*

7.30 A broad measure of agreement in principle exists on desirable objectives for professional education. A series of detailed proposals have been put forward by the CIC and others for implementation. The CIC is best placed to co-ordinate action, if necessary involving advisers from the Departments for Education and Employment and DOE. A task force should be set up to supervise the delivery of the action points which have already been proposed, according to clear and published timescales. Clients, contractors and specialists are also very interested in this, and should be informed of progress through the Implementation Forum.

Research & Development

The Problem

7.31 There is widespread concern within the industry at the level of investment in research and development. This was identified as a serious issue in "Building Towards 2001", which added that the low or nonexistent level of profitability within the contracting sector left little funding for such vital activity. Investment comes mainly from public bodies (some of which have since been privatised such as the water industry) or from manufacturers/suppliers. Some very valuable projects have also been commissioned and funded by clients[64]. But a recent Discussion Document[65] by a CIC working party expressed the view that "UK spending on construction research and its dissemination is substantially below that judged necessary by a succession of authoritative studies".

7.32 As with other construction industry problems, the United Kingdom is not alone in its disappointing level of R & D investment. The EC/W S Atkins report found that, within the EU, "The total level of construction research is low, and needs to be raised nearer to the average of other industries. The EU spends much less than Japan on construction R&D". It advocated that "R&D expenditure on construction needs to be increased from its present level of about 0.1% of GDP to at least match the average of other sectors, around 0.2% of GDP and must be shared by Government, industry and clients. This would be equivalent to 2 - 3% of construction industry turnover". The United Kingdom appears to be a very long way from either target at present, although it did achieve the 0.1% figure throughout the 1980s[66]. The Institution of Civil Engineers, quoting a DOE analysis, says that "the comparable ratios for France and Germany are 50% higher than the UK while the Japanese ratio is five times greater", and comments "this poor performance does not augur well for the future competitiveness of UK contractors and consulting engineers in terms of their improved productivity leading to reductions in basic cost" (ICE evidence, November 1993).

---

[64] See "Profit from Innovation", CIC, 1993. Several Universities and other Institutions are heavily involved in client funded research. The development of the Centre for Window and Cladding Technology at Bath University is a highly praised initiative.

[65] "Private Funding for Construction Innovation and Research - Options for a National Initiative, a Discussion Paper", prepared by a Working Party of the CIC Research & Development Committee, CIC, January 1994.

[66] In a recent lecture, Dr Peter Bransby, the Director General of CIRIA, estimated that the UK's current investment on R&D is around 0.03% of output. (Unwin Lecture at the ICE, April 1994.)

7.33 There are some specific problems relating to the United Kingdom research programme. The Director General of CIRIA pointed out:

1. "The fragmented nature of construction is such that individual companies cannot appropriate the benefits of investment in such research, especially that to do with the construction process and the integration of design and construction. For this reason, while there is some investment in confidential research by individual companies, especially material producers, whose results will be exploited commercially by those companies, there is little investment in research which is of general benefit."

2. Regarding technology transfer, "Those active in the dissemination of information ... do not appropriate the benefit." (Letter from Dr Peter Bransby, November 1993.)

7.34 In its evidence, the Concrete Society reports that only about 10% of current research on concrete is geared towards improvements in productivity and quality. It has sought to establish a new industry wide focus for identifying and promoting market-led developments, through the formation of a Technical Development Board of key industry leaders from the concrete sector. A development strategy is now being proposed which gives a high priority to improved dissemination of information to "ensure that industry at the sharp end gains competitive edge and value for money from its use of concrete".

Research Strategy

7.35 The DOE will fund about £23 million in research in 1994/5. It has also formed a panel with the CIC, the CIEC and the CLG to develop a "whole industry research strategy". That panel met for the first time in March, and is intended to ensure that the research carried out in the public and private sectors is relevant and also disseminated in a practical way. The Construction Industry European Research Club, launched by Mr Tony Baldry MP on 10th May and to be managed by the Building Research Establishment (BRE), is another new initiative aimed at encouraging greater participation by UK companies in the European Union's research and development programme. The BRE also provides the secretariat for the International Association for Automation and Robotics in Construction. The Science and Engineering Research Council's new innovation manufacturing initiative, which has been taken over by the Engineering and Physical Sciences Research Council, identifies construction as a sector needing specific attention. A new LINK programme "Integration in design and construction" has recently been approved. These are all highly worthwhile projects. But active attempts should be made by the DOE to involve clients in all of them, as the CIPS final report recommends. It is also important that these various initiatives should be monitored by the DOE to ensure that they are co-ordinated and delivering effective results.

7.36 The CIC's Discussion Document concludes, as does the EC/W S Atkins report, that about another 0.1% of UK construction output is required, or about an additional £40 million, in respect of construction research of general benefit and subsequent technology transfer. It examines various methods of financing such sums. There are precedents for levies for construction research around the world, including New Zealand, Belgium, Sweden and Florida (USA). In considering different options, the Discussion Document chose a charge based upon pay-roll, possibly collected by the CITB. This proposal for a mandatory levy to finance research is far from new. Similar proposals were put forward in the Woodbine Parish[67], Muir-Wood[68], Sallabank[69], ICE[70] and Derbyshire[71] reports between 1964 and 1992. The case is also persuasively argued by Dr Bransby in his Unwin Memorial lecture in April 1994 (see footnote 66) where he says that "it is an idea whose time has come". But not everyone agrees. The CIEC final report mentions "only limited support within CIEC for a research levy".

7.37 It is clear that voluntary contributions are not meeting the R&D need. But I doubt whether the CITB is the right vehicle for collecting a levy. The purpose of that organisation is training for the construction industry, not research and development. The CITB's role has always provoked some controversy, especially amongst smaller firms or those from specialist trades who feel they pay out in levy more than they can expect to receive back in grant. Significant sectors of the construction industry are outside the CITB scope. The CIC Document also suggests that consultants should be brought within the levy system, but accepts that their contribution needs further thought. Consultants are not within CITB scope either.

7.38 To raise the £40 million proposed by the CIC and EC/W S Atkins report for research and development would be a large task. It requires further study and debate. The Implementation Forum may wish to discuss whether that target is in practice necessary or realistic. The problem is not so much identifying the possible routes for a levy. That has been done in many of the reports and surveys already undertaken. The difficulty is to choose which of them will be:-

1. even handed between the different sections of the process, and fairly spread between them so that they can actually afford the levy; and

2. sufficiently robust to produce a large sum of money on a consistent basis, and with a widespread level of acceptance.

---

[67] *"Building Research and Information Services", 1964 MPBW.*

[68] *"Civil Engineering Task Force", 1981, SERC, DOE and DOT.*

[69] *"Strategy for Construction R&D", 1985, NEDO.*

[70] *"Construction Research and Development Reports", 1986-1992, ICE.*

[71] *"Research and Development in the UK Construction Industry", 1990, Sir Andrew Derbyshire for NEDO.*

7.39   A new feedback research and information initiative would be much less costly. The introduction of mandatory "BUILD" insurance would be a major factor (see Chapter 11).   If the insurance companies became heavily involved in providing ten year cover for commercial contracts in the building sector, they might wish to take steps to raise quality in the industry.   In France, an agency[72] exists which charges a statutory levy on insurance premiums.   The levy is used to improve quality in construction and to publish best practice information.   Such a system could be incorporated within the United Kingdom structures, and would provide a potential source of additional finance for a research and information initiative.   The annual amount collected through the levy in France is about £2.5 million (source: CIC Discussion Paper).   The receipts from a similar system in the UK would reflect the percentage set as levy.   There may be an enhanced role for EU funding and co-ordination for construction research, as suggested in the EC/W S Atkins report.   There is also a case for making information regarding the contribution made by a company to research and development part of the qualification system for the national register (see Chapter 6).

Recommendations 23.1 to 23.4: Research and Development

7.40   Expenditure on research and development in the industry is generally thought to be inadequate and dissemination of it faces real difficulties.

1.   The DOE should take steps to involve clients in its existing research strategy programme.

2.   Since a number of initiatives have been launched, they should be monitored by the DOE to ensure that they are co-ordinated and deliver effective results.

3.   There is insufficient consensus yet for any specific levy route to raise a large sum for research. This needs further discussion by the Implementation Forum, who should also discuss what a realistic financial target would be.

4   A new research and information initiative aimed at providing timely and relevant good practice feedback should be initiated through funding by a levy on the premia for mandatory "BUILD" type insurance, as proposed in Chapter 11.

Quality Assurance

7.41   Every client has the right to expect high quality from the project which it has commissioned. But unfortunately that is by no means always the outcome. The Building Research Establishment (BRE), in conjunction with a number of sponsors, launched the Construction Quality Forum (CQF) last November, arising directly out of a

---

[72] *"L'Agence pour la prévention des désordres et l'amélioration de la qualité de la Construction", founded in 1983, and representing public authorities, insurance companies and "toutes les familles du bâtiment" - clients, consultants and contractors.*

recommendation in "Building Towards 2001", that "a database of defects should be maintained". At the launch, BRE reported that "each year, defects or failures in design and construction cost members of the construction industry more than £1000 million". Despite this depressing statistic, very few clients were represented at the launch of the CQF. The CIPS final report recommends that clients should contribute to the CQF and use its database to assist in the selection of designers and contractors. I would endorse that recommendation, which should be seen in conjunction with my proposals for CMIS and ConReg.

7.42 BS5750 certification has been increasingly taken up within the industry process. But it is not unanimously supported. "Building Towards 2001", while welcoming its widespread adoption, commented that BS5750 had "met with practical difficulties when being implemented in the project environment", and asked if the Standard addressed "the real issues of quality of the product and the operational methods of achieving it on a construction project". Other comments have included:-

1. "There is much debate within the industry as to the cost effectiveness of BS5750, particularly in relation to smaller companies..... Many companies view the cost of accreditation as an unnecessary overhead which is not really relevant for the type of business they carry out" (SECG final report).

2. "BS5750 is a very significant step in the right direction but it does not assure "quality" in the old fashioned meaning of the word. The proper selection of advisers, consultants, main contractors and subcontractors .... is still the only way to get the right quality" (Ground Forum evidence, March 1994).

3. "BS5750 was designed to ensure that specified standards of quality management are achieved.....It does not ensure that good standards are set in the first place" (CIPS final report).

7.43 A report was commissioned in 1993 by CIRIA into "Quality Management in Construction - survey of experiences with BS5750". That report and survey, carried out by a firm of quantity surveyors, has not yet been published. The draft report found "no evidence to suggest that BS5750 is not relevant to the construction industry or any individual organisation related to the industry", but also found mixed results and responses from the firms surveyed.

7.44 Some have pointed out that even if a main contractor was quality assured, it did not mean that the subcontractors undertaking much of the construction work on site also were. The Ground Forum commented that "if clients are serious about quality, they should be prepared to call tenders only from quality assured firms which they have selected at least on quality grounds. They must also insist that specialist subcontractors appointed by their main contractor are also quality assured" (evidence, March 1994).

7.45 BS5750 can play a useful part in helping firms to have good management and administrative procedures. The qualification form for CMIS asks if the applicant firm has such certification, as also does the Department of Transport. Improving management procedures at all levels is vital for the industry's performance, and needs to be part of a drive towards Total Quality Management (TQM)[73]. TQM is not solely about procedures. In his study of TQM, Ron Baden Hellard emphasises certain aspects which lie at the heart

---

[73] *The Henderson Committee, which was set up by the DTI in 1992 under the chairmanship of Sir Denys Henderson, to study the feasibility of improving the performance of British industry through TQM, adopted the working definition: "Total quality management is a way of managing an organisation to ensure the satisfaction at every stage of the needs and expectations of both internal and external customers-that is, shareholders, consumers of its goods and services, employees and the community in which it operates - by means of every job, every process being carried out right, first time and every time".*

of this Report. He stresses that the "philosophy of teamwork and co-operation, not confrontation and conflict, is long overdue".[74] Some contractors are making real attempts to improve quality and introduce TQM. (For example, Bovis provided some excellent examples to the Review of their internal guidance for staff which are intended to improve performance and encourage team building, and implement Project Quality Planning - a TQM approach for post competitive tender partnerships.) These efforts should be encouraged by leading clients, firms and Government.

7.46 Quality assurance certification should continue to be encouraged within the construction industry as a potentially useful tool for improving corporate management systems. But more evidence is needed that it will also raise standards of site performance and project delivery before it should be made a qualification condition for consideration for public sector work. The implementation stage of this Review should try to achieve a consensus from the industry and professions as to how BS5750 accreditation can improve project delivery and site performance as well as office management systems. Encouraging a Total Quality approach should pervade the whole implementation phase. It should involve heavy emphasis upon teamwork and co-operation.

A Productivity Initiative

7.47 All the proposals in this Chapter, and those designed to improve procurement performance in other Chapters, will have an effect on productivity. The "Towards 2001" report recommended setting up a National Construction Productivity Centre as a research and information dissemination agency. The recession has prevented that happening on cost grounds. But BRE and CIRIA have now formed a Construction Productivity Network, as a low cost information exchange facility. While that is commendable, more action is needed, and monitoring of improvements. Both the CIPS and Professor John Bennett of Reading University have recommended a target of reducing real construction costs by 30 per cent over five years[75].

Recommendation 24: Productivity Target

7.48 This target of 30 per cent real cost reduction by the year 2000 should be accepted by Ministers and the industry, and it should be the duty of the Implementation Forum to encourage, assist and monitor progress towards its achievement. This will involve early agreement on a benchmarking system. If a Construction Industry Development Agency (see Chapter 12) is set up, meeting this target should be its key task.

---

[74] *"Total Quality in Construction Projects" by Ron Baden Hellard, published by Thomas Telford Services Ltd, 1993.*

[75] *CIPS final report, and speech by Professor Bennett to the CIPS Conference, 30th March 1994.*
I am very grateful to Professor Bennett and his colleagues for their useful advice on several aspects of this Review.

8.1   The work of the Review has not been only about disputes between main contractors and specialist/trade (sub) contractors[76]. It is, however, those which have generated most heat and correspondence. Some main contractors have said that they have no real problems, and that relations with subcontractors are generally good. Doubtless that is the case with some firms and some sites. If it were always so, my post bag would have been much lighter, and the Review much quicker. But it is not always so.

8.2   The most persuasive evidence in this regard was provided for me by a national contracting firm. The company commissioned a survey in August 1993 from an independent survey team[77]. The survey questioned a sample of subcontractors, representative of most major trades, size, volume of work with the company, and geographic region. It included a small number of subcontractors who were reluctant to bid for work with the company, or had failed to win work recently. All those questioned were aware that the company had commissioned the survey. The questions included the most controversial issues between main contractors and subcontractors, such as:

1.   Are your tenders dealt with fairly?

2.   Does the company indulge in Dutch Auctions or similar practices?

3.   How comfortable are you with the main contractor's terms and conditions? (The company has its own subcontract form.)

4.   Are you fairly treated on financial matters?

5.   Are contra-charges handled properly?

6.   Do you feel part of the team?

8.3   The interviewees were asked to score each of the answers against a prescribed 1 to 10 rating system. 7 was "acceptable", 6 "fair", 5 "poor". Below 5 was "very unsatisfactory", 8 was "better than acceptable, good" and 9 "very good". Most importantly, benchmarking was undertaken against other main contractors. The results showed:-

1.   Only on the answers to the final questions - such as the overall reputation of the company and hoping to work with them again - did it rate better than acceptable, good (8.3).

2.   Its ratings on post bid as a whole were below acceptable (6.0) as was the answer regarding dutch auctioning (5.8).

---

[76]   *Even the terminology is a matter of dispute! The JCT, ICE and GC/Works/1 Standard Forms use the expression "subcontractor". The SEACC system uses "specialist contractor". Specialists who are involved in design work tend to differentiate between themselves and "trade contractors" who are not.*

[77]   *The identity of the company, and the people who carried out the survey, must remain anonymous. The company also undertook a separate survey in Scotland. The results were similar, though more favourable. The company's mean rating was 7.2, the average of the 7 competitors considered was 6.9. The score of 7 was "acceptable".*

3. Most interviewees were very uncomfortable with the company's terms and conditions (5.2), with contra-charging particularly criticised (4.8).

4. The overall mean rating of company across all sections of the survey was below acceptable (6.8).

5. The company did better than its combined competitors (6.5). Table 13 compares the results, with the company being the bold line and the combined competitors the other line.

TABLE 13: THE COMPANY VERSUS ITS COMBINED COMPETITORS: TREATMENT OF SPECIALISTS

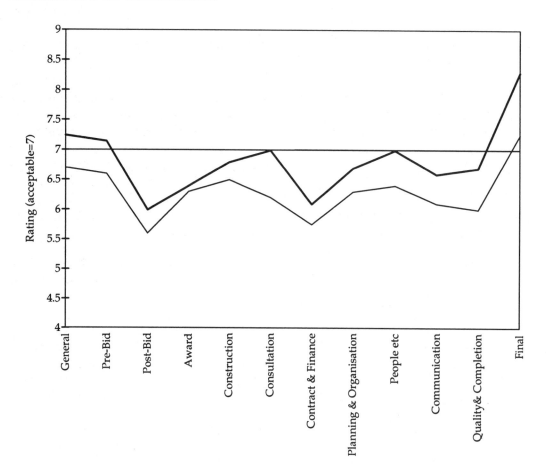

8.4   The survey conclusions were:

1. "If [we are] truly to become an excellent company, the appraisal of our performance by specialist contractors is a key indicator. In almost all areas the company is seen to perform below an "acceptable" level."

2. "It is an industry problem. Where we are better, so are our competitors. Where we score poorly, so do others. Inherently the industry "macho" culture, where we reward crisis management and "screw the subbie", is at fault."

3. "This attitude does not motivate specialist contractors to perform at their highest levels."

4. "The performance of specialist subcontractors is crucial to the success of our organisation. If we can improve the quality of support we give to specialists, then the quality of product and service will be measurably superior... It will also reduce conflict."

8.5 The report (written by a senior University lecturer) went on to recommend that the company should:

1. Develop better relations through partnering or partnership arrangements.

2. Involve subcontractors earlier to achieve project objectives, and develop greater team involvement through the project life cycle and beyond.

3. Utilise the skill and knowledge of the subcontractors more fully and better, and recognise that subcontractors can and want to make a greater contribution.

4. Develop a more structured, standardised and ethical approach to the procurement and management of subcontractors.

(Source: survey for the company on the level of satisfaction of specialist contractors in dealing with it, both main report and executive summary, 1993)

8.6 That report and its conclusions speak for themselves. The intention behind the survey was commendable and is part of a drive by that company to improve its own performance for clients. It indicates a real and progressive attempt to examine that company's relationship with its subcontractors and how this might be improved. Such feedback provides a valuable resource and other firms should carry out similar surveys. Further detailed work, including survey results carried out amongst specialist/trade contractors in the Autumn of 1992, will be set out in the report of a project for CIRIA currently being finalised by the Centre for Strategic Studies in Construction, University of Reading, assisted by Sir Alexander Gibb & Partners Limited.[78]

8.7 The problems of this contentious area were set out in the Interim Report. The commercial realities are well known. Teamwork cannot be achieved unless all sections of the process are committed to it. That must include:-

1. **Clients,** who vary in their interest. Some, including some Government Departments, display no discernible interest in subcontractors. Other clients take an intense interest in all participants on and off site, for the reasons set out above. Some clients go to considerable lengths to brief subcontractors and their operatives on-site to ensure that they feel fully part of the construction team.

2. **Consultants,** on whatever basis they are retained and under whatever procurement route, especially as they often seek to transfer responsibility for detailed design to specialists.

3. **Main contractors,** whose role in pulling together the performance of the contract is crucial. Some evidence has argued that main contractors no longer have a necessary role in the modern construction industry or even that their influence is malign. I do not agree. They remain the most effective mobilisers and co-ordinators of resources. They are responsible for the smooth running of the whole site throughout its operation, and for the performance and quality of the work of all their domestic subcontractors.

4. **Specialist/trade contractors,** many of whom (particularly specialists) also employ sub subcontractors. Some of the smallest subcontractors, including those at the very end of the construction process such as landscape companies or those responsible for road lining, have a particular sense of grievance at their

---

[78] *"Guide to Effective Specialist and Trade Contracting" by Gray, Hughes and Murdoch, currently unpublished report for CIRIA.*

treatment. Some smaller specialist engineering contractors complained, both directly and through the Confederation of Construction Specialists, about the onerous contract conditions which they received from larger engineering specialists to whom they were in subcontract relationship.

8.8 I have already described the necessary action in other vital areas:-

1. The client deciding upon the project and contract strategy, and an effective brief being prepared.

2. Implementing the desired procurement route, and choosing the team to do so, including fair methods of remunerating them and ensuring effective performance.

3. Following responsible qualification and tendering procedures, drawing upon registered contractors and subcontractors.

4. Appropriate contract conditions, based on teamwork and "win-win" principles.

Recommendation 25: Unfair Conditions

8.9 If the NEC (including its accompanying subcontract), following suggested amendments, is adopted as a normal procurement route for most construction work, or if the Standard Forms of the JCT and the CCSJC are amended to conform with the principles which I have suggested, many of the concerns expressed by clients, main contractors and subcontractors will be met. All parties in the construction process should then be encouraged to use those Standard Forms without amendment. To aid confidence and promote the use of such forms, their central provisions should be underpinned by legislation. This might best be done by a "Construction Contracts Bill" which extended inter alia unfair contracts legislation. The Bill should state that where one of the above Standard Forms (including subcontracts) is used, the following actions should be unfair or invalid:

1. any attempt to amend or delete the sections relating to times and conditions of payment, including the right of interest on late payment;

2. to seek to deny or frustrate the right of immediate adjudication to any party to the contract or subcontract, where it has been requested by that party (see also Chapter 9);

3. to refuse to implement the decision of the adjudicator;

4. to seek to exercise any right of set-off or contra charge without:

    a. giving notification in advance;

    b. specifying the exact reason for deducting the set-off; and

    c. being prepared to submit immediately to adjudication and accepting the result, subject to (3) above;

5. to seek to set-off in respect of any contract other than the one in progress.

8.10 Some clients and contractors may still continue to use bespoke forms, even when generally acceptable Standard Forms have become available in accordance with this Report's recommendations. Points (2) to (5) above should therefore be declared unfair and invalid for all construction contracts (ie not only when Standard Forms are used). In addition, any attempt by a contractor to include a clause in a bespoke form with the effect of introducing "pay-when-paid" conditions should be explicitly declared unfair and invalid.

8.11 Legislative provision should also be made (though this might be done by other means than unfair contract terms legislation) that clients should set up a secure trust fund. Details of this are contained in Chapter 10.

9.1 "During the past 50 years much of the United States construction environment has been degraded from one of a positive relationship between all members of the project team to a contest consumed in fault finding and defensiveness which results in litigation. The industry has become extremely adversarial and we are paying the price... If the construction industry is to become less adversarial, we must reexamine the construction process, particularly the relationship between contractor/subcontractor. A positive alliance of these parties constitutes an indispensable link to a successful project... Disputes will continue as long as people fail to trust one another." (Newsletter from "The Dispute Avoidance and Resolution Task Force", (Dart), Washington D.C., February 1994.)

9.2 The UK construction industry is not alone in having adversarial attitudes. But the United States has taken positive steps to try to reduce them, with the growth of Alternative Dispute Resolution (ADR). The debate over adjudication, conciliation/mediation and arbitration has been very strong throughout this Review. There has been growing consensus over the action needed.

9.3 The best solution is to avoid disputes. If procedures relating to procurement and tendering are improved, the causes of conflict will be reduced. If a contract document is adopted which places the emphasis on teamwork and partnership to solve problems, that is another major step. The prepricing of variations is also important.

Adjudication

9.4 Nevertheless disputes may arise, despite everyone's best efforts to avoid them. A contract form with a built in adjudication process provides a clear route[79]. If a dispute cannot be resolved first by the parties themselves in good faith, it is referred to the adjudicator for decision. Such a system must become the key to settling disputes in the construction industry. Separate adjudication is not currently provided for within JCT 80. The architect has the specific role of contract administrator there and is under a professional duty to act impartially as between employer and contractor. This was considered at length by a working party which reported to the Joint Contracts Tribunal in 1993. It made proposals for clauses in the contract providing for mediation and/or adjudication. It spelt out how those clauses should work, and what form of disputes they should include. Other than lack of agreement within the JCT, there has been nothing to prevent the introduction of such procedures within JCT 80 already.

9.5 If the NEC becomes normal construction contract documentation, its procedures for adjudication will be followed, though they may require some amendments. But adjudication should be incorporated forthwith within the JCT family as a whole. (Regarding the JCT Minor Works Form, under which work tends to be fairly quickly carried out, the Tribunal may prefer to incorporate a similar conciliation procedure to that in the

---

[79] *The SEACC system contains a particularly good model for adjudication. The Interim Report set out in detail those other contracts which have adjudication or conciliation. There is also some provision within subcontract forms.*

ICE Minor Works Form, though there is no inherent reason why adjudication should not be used for any size of contract.) There should be no restriction on the issues to be placed before the adjudicator for decision, and no specified "cooling off period" before the adjudicator can be called in. The adjudicator should be named in the contract before work starts but called in when necessary.[80] The adjudicator must be neutral. If agreement cannot be reached by the parties themselves on a name, or names[81], an appointment should be made by the Presidents of one of the appropriate professional bodies. Either party to a dispute should have the right to ask for adjudication. As well as dealing with disputes between clients and main contractors, the contract documents must specify that the adjudicator must have equal scope to determine disputes between contractors and subcontractors, and between subcontractors and sub subcontractors. Jurisdiction on subcontract issues should not be limited to disputes over set off. It should encompass any matter which can also be within the scope of resolution under the main contract. (In many cases, disputes between clients and main contractors also involve subcontractors.) The adjudicator's fee should initially be the responsibility of the party calling in the adjudicator, but the adjudicator should subsequently apportion it as appropriate. Both main contractors and subcontractors have pressed hard for such a system to be standard procedure for dispute resolution. They should now seek to make it effective, in a spirit of teamwork.

9.6   It is crucial that adjudication decisions should be implemented at once. Mr Roger Knowles, Chairman of James R Knowles, Construction Contracts Consultants, writes:- "A well drafted disputes procedure involving adjudicators and arbitrators operating in an unrestricted manner will help disputes to be resolved quickly and inexpensively. For disputes settled by these methods, appeals and reference to the High Court should not be permitted under any circumstances, as it is the constant spectre of appeal which conditions the manner in which many arbitrations are conducted and which has emasculated the whole process". (Paper by Mr Knowles, April 1994.)

9.7   I have considered this proposal. It has also been made by others, who have drawn specific attention to the role of the expert under IChemE conditions. It is correct that the authority of the adjudicator/expert must be upheld, and that the decisions should be implemented at once. Such published experience as exists of adjudication - and it does not seem very extensive at main contract level, because the possibility of the system being used appears to induce the parties to reach their own settlement without recourse to it - suggests that it is successful in reducing disputes without further appeal or litigation[82]. But it would be difficult to deny a party which feels totally aggrieved by an adjudicator's decision any opportunity to appeal either to the courts or arbitration. I doubt whether such a restriction would be enforceable. The SEACC system, which generally defers access to the courts until after acceptance, allows such an earlier reference to the courts in certain specified and limited circumstances. However:

---

[80] *Some evidence suggested that for small and medium sized contracts there is no need to name an adjudicator in advance, but the contract document must provide for a method of appointing one if the need arises. (This suggestion is made in the Building Structures Group's final report to the Review.) On balance, I believe it would be better if the adjudicator was named even for the smallest contract, but, if not, the provisions must allow for a nominee to be appointed immediately on request. It would be damaging if the appointment of the adjudicator was frustrated by delay or disagreement by one of the parties to the dispute.*

[81] *Medium or large sized projects may require more than one name for different areas of possible dispute. Alternatively, a multi-disciplinary firm or firms could be named.*

[82] *See for example the article by Mr Michael Morris in the February edition of the Journal of the Institute of Arbitrators about Adjudication Procedures on the Dartford River Crossing, and "Adjudicators, Experts and Keeping Out of Court" by Mr Mark C. McGaw of Lovell, White, Durrant which appeared in Construction Law Journal, 1992.*

1. The adjudication result must be implemented at once, even if it is subsequently overturned by the courts or an arbitrator after practical completion. If the award of the adjudicator involves payment, it must be made at once. Placing the money in the hands of an impartial stakeholder should only be permitted with the specific agreement of all the parties in the dispute, or if the adjudicator (exceptionally) so directs.

2. The courts (unless there is some exceptional and immediate issue of law which must be brought in front of a Judge/Official Referee at once) should only be approached as a last resort and after practical completion of the contract.

Conciliation and Mediation

9.8 Mediation/conciliation is another route of Alternative Dispute Resolution. It is a voluntary, non-binding process, intended to bring the parties to agreement. A mediator has no powers of enforcement or of making a binding recommendation. Some contracts which contain a conciliation[83] procedure seem to work well - the ICE Minor Works Contract is its best selling document with "many satisfied customers".[84] Mediation/conciliation should contain two crucial provisions.

1. The scope of the conciliation must cover all potential aspects of dispute, and that scope must be fully stepped down into subcontracts.

2. It must also be a condition of contract that such provisions are fully available to both main contractor and subcontractors without deletion, amendment or restriction.

Most disputes on site are, I believe, better resolved by speedy decision - i.e. adjudication - rather than by a mediation procedure in which the parties reach their own settlement.

Multi-Tiered A.D.R.

9.9 Some very large projects may require more than one form of dispute resolution. That section of the Hong Kong Airport Core Programme which is the Government's responsibility (basically the infrastructure and related projects) has a four tier level of dispute resolution - engineer's decision, mandatory mediation/conciliation, adjudication and arbitration.[85] It is to be hoped that such complex procedures would only be required to be used rarely. But it is proper that they should be available in such massive contracts, and special conditions attached to the form of contract could accommodate them. Some have suggested that it would be appropriate that the adjudicator should be a 3 person board for large projects, with one representative from each side of the dispute, and an independent chairperson. Such a board would need to be differently constructed if the

---

[83] *The CIEC report says that the ICE Conciliation Procedure is currently being revised to place more emphasis on reaching an agreed solution.*

[84] *Source: Letter from Mr Guy Cottam, February 1994.*

[85] *The airport itself has a two tier procedure - decision of the project director and arbitration. The airport railway has engineer's decision, mediation and arbitration. (Source: Masons, providing a paper by Mr Michael Byrne of the Government secretariat.)*

dispute was between client and contractor than if it was between contractor and subcontractor, let alone a dispute between client and contractor to which subcontractors were joined. My view is that the board should all be independent, and a panel of names should be in the contract to deal with all major disputes. Dispute review boards have proved successful in the United States.

Arbitration

9.10 Arbitrators are an expert and dedicated group of people, with whom I have had constructive discussions during the Review. Many of them also serve now as conciliators or experts, and in other forms of Alternative Dispute Resolution, and they may form a core resource for the adjudication system. As stated in the Interim Report, there is considerable dissatisfaction with arbitration within the construction industry because of its perceived complexity, slowness and expense. The arbitrators themselves favour reforms to the procedures which will allow for less formality and speedier hearings[86]. Following the report of a Committee under the chairmanship of Lord Justice Steyn, the Department of Trade & Industry has published a draft Bill and consultation paper which seeks to clarify and consolidate the law (February 1994). Arbitration has a continuing part to play in dispute resolution within the construction industry. But it should be a last resort after practical completion, if a party to a dispute remains aggrieved by the decision of the adjudicator even though that decision has already been implemented. If the proposed system of adjudication works properly, many current arbitrators will be making decisions during the course of the project, but in the role of adjudicators, which is what many of them would wish to be able to do now. There are provisions for speedy arbitration hearings during the course of the contract under rule 7 of the JCT Arbitration Rules 1988. But the experience of arbitrators themselves is that they are little used. Full arbitration after the completion of the contract will, hopefully, become much rarer.

Interim Payments, Adjudication and the Courts

9.11 Concern has also been expressed to me about the operation of Supreme Court Rules 14 and 29 relating to Summary Judgement or interim payment of awards. The Official Referees Solicitors Association (ORSA) has made proposals about interim payments:-

1   The amount of any interim payment should be the court's best estimate at that stage of the amount for which the plaintiff would succeed, taking account of any serious cross claims by the defendant which might be sustained.

2   If the court is unable to make an adequate estimate, it could refer the matter for report by a Court Adjudicator, whose recommendation would normally be accepted.

(Source: Discussion Paper by ORSA, "Interim Payment Awards in Building Contract Cases", July 1992.)

---

[86] *Evidence by the Chartered Institute of Arbitrators, January 1994.*

9.12 The draft Arbitration Bill published by the DTI also contains, in clause 14, proposals for possible interim payments. However, the wording of subclause (1) requires the arbitrator (or "tribunal") to be "satisfied" that the respondent will be found liable to pay to the claimant a sum at least equal to the amount of the interim payment. If the arbitrator acts in practice as the courts have done over RSC Orders 14 and 29, the likelihood is that few such awards would be made. Clause 14 (3) of the draft Bill would also allow the parties to omit such provisions by agreement. The commercial dominance of some parties in construction contracts suggests that it is better not to have clauses which "allow" participants to opt out of fair dispute resolution procedures.

9.13 Recourse to the courts or arbitration should become less frequent because of other changes which I have recommended to procurement practice, contract conditions, tighter restrictions over set-off and the introduction of adjudicators as a normal procedure for settling disputes. The detailed working of the Courts of Justice, of which the Official Referees are a distinguished part, is not a matter on which I feel competent to make recommendations. Very senior judges have stressed that holding up the flow of cash is bad for the construction industry[87]. If adjudication is introduced as the normal method of dispute resolution in construction, the courts will perhaps take account of the wishes of the industry to ensure that cash does flow speedily. But one regrettable possibility could be if a party to an adjudication refused to honour the award of the adjudicator immediately, or even to discuss the use of stake holders, despite being bound to do so. In such circumstances, the party to whom the award had been made should be able to approach the Official Referee immediately and obtain a judgement for payment under an expedited procedure as suggested by ORSA, be it under Rules 14 or 29, or any other appropriate legal provision. It would be fatal to the adjudication system if one party successfully attempted to use greater financial strength to exhaust the other by delays in settlement. The courts should have a role to support the adjudication system in such circumstances.

Recommendations 26.1 - 26. 5: Adjudication

9.14 I have already recommended that a system of adjudication should be introduced within all the Standard Forms of Contract (except where comparable arrangements already exist for mediation or conciliation) and that this should be underpinned by legislation. I also recommend that:-

1. There should be no restrictions on the issues capable of being referred to the adjudicator, conciliator or mediator, either in the main contract or subcontract documentation.

2. The award of the adjudicator should be implemented immediately. The use of stake holders should only be permitted if both parties agree or if the adjudicator so directs.

3. Any appeals to arbitration or the courts should be after practical completion, and should not be permitted to delay the implementation of the award, unless an immediate and exceptional issue arises for the courts or as in the circumstances described in (4) overleaf.

---

[87] C/f Lord Justice Lawton "The Courts are aware of what happens in these building disputes; cases go either to arbitration or before an Official Referee; they drag on and on; the cash flow is held up....that sort of result is to be avoided if possible" (Ellis Mechanical Services -v-. Wates Construction Limited, 1976, 2BLR 57).

4. Resort to the courts should be immediately available if a party refuses to implement the award of an adjudicator. In such circumstances, the courts may wish to support the system of adjudication by agreeing to expedited procedures for interim payments.

5. Training procedures should be devised for adjudicators. A Code of Practice should also be drawn up under the auspices of the proposed Implementation Forum.

10.1   The cascade system of payment in the industry - normally client to main contractor, main contractor to subcontractor, and so on down the chain[88] - makes the exposure of different parts of the process to the insolvency of one participant particularly serious. The chain may begin above the client, with the banks or other funders who are financing the project. If a main contractor fails, subcontractors will be treated as unsecured creditors in respect of work which they have already carried out (or purchased equipment), whether on or off site. Even their retention monies will be at risk, since domestic subcontracts make no provision for secure trust funds. In theory, nominated subcontractors are protected in respect of their retention monies because the employer is supposed to hold the money in a fiduciary capacity. Also protected in theory is the main contractor's retention, in the event of the failure of the employer (c/f JCT 80, Clause 30.5). But:

1.   Some forms of contract do not keep retention as "trust monies", either for the contractor or for nominated subcontractors. Even some Standard Forms do not, (e.g. ICE 6th edition).

2.   Some employers delete these provisions - including public sector clients, on the grounds that they will not become insolvent.

3.   The onus of establishing if the trust accounts have been set up rests in practice on the contractor or nominated subcontractor.

10.2   The normal interim payments for work performed are also insecure. The case of British Eagle International Airlines -v- Compagnie Nationale Air France (1975) - which led to changes to JCT 80 from the previous limited protection in JCT 63 - removed the right of the employer to pay nominated subcontractors directly if the main contractor failed. The practical reality now, if the main contractor becomes insolvent, is that the primary or secured creditors of the main contractor will receive some monies which are intended for and owing to the subcontractor for work carried out. If the client fails, the main contractor and potentially also the subcontractors will be disadvantaged.

10.3   It is absolutely fundamental to trust within the construction industry that participants should be paid for the work which they have undertaken. It may be argued that there is no need for any action because:

1.   Clients may exercise responsible prequalification procedures to ensure that work is only awarded to stable firms. They can also insist upon knowing who the subcontractors are, or they can nominate or "name" them, so as to prevent disruption of the work through failure there.

2.   Equally, contractors (or subcontractors) can decline to work for a client (or main contractor) or can require prepayment or bonds/indemnities from them.

3.   All businesses in all industries are at risk if insolvency affects their clients. Bad debt is not only a problem in construction and it is possible to insure against it.

---

[88] *The Building Employers Confederation have identified a site with nine layers of subcontractors!*

10.4   Such arguments ignore the practical realities of construction. However diligently clients, contractors or subcontractors check on each other, the causes of the failure of any participant may be unrelated to the particular contract, or even to work in this country. In a difficult trading climate for construction, firms will undertake work for low (or no) margins, and will not endanger their chances of being selected by demanding prepayment or indemnities, even if they are aware that there might be a payment problem. Bad debt insurance is possible, but it is another cost overhead at a time when most firms are cutting their overheads in order to reduce their quotations for "preliminaries" and remain competitive.

10.5   The construction industry has a unique characteristic. Its goods and services become part of the land once incorporated within the building, and thus the property of the landowner. Any "retention of title" clause devised by suppliers or contractors who are delivering materials to site ceases to protect them once the materials are incorporated within the works. In construction, the contractor is likely to be well down the queue for payment if the employer fails, behind the funders or others who have charges on the land. There is specific construction industry legislation in a number of countries to deal with this potential injustice. The most comprehensive is the Ontario Construction Lien Act 1983, but there are others even more recent.

10.6   An effective way to deal with this problem is by setting up trust accounts for interim payments (and also retentions, if the latter system continues). I have already recommended such trust accounts as a necessary Core Clause to the New Engineering Contract. They should also be built into other construction contract conditions and should be underpinned by legislation.

10.7   Action was taken in Germany last year. The previous arrangement under the German Civil Code (Section 648) was that a contractor or trade contractor was able to demand a mortgage on land on which work was being carried out by the firm. This was, in effect, a Builder's Lien system. However, it proved an unsatisfactory remedy because a charge did little to help subcontractors, and was usually displaced by a prior charge registered by a bank or financial institution. The 1993 Contractors Security Law provides that German contractors can demand from their employers "adequate security" for the balance of any money payable to them under the contract. These rights also extend to consultants and subcontractors, but not suppliers. Public authorities are exempt. The right to demand secure payment is statutory and cannot be excluded by contract. It is in practice to be achieved through bank guarantees or surety bonds, (but not on-demand bonds) with a maximum cost to the beneficiary of 2% per annum of the value of the surety. (Any excess cost is to be met by the provider.) Failure by the employer or the main contractor to provide adequate security allows the main contractor or the subcontractor the right to suspend the works immediately, or, ultimately, to terminate. Most of the larger German contractors have close links with banks and so have no difficulty in providing security. Smaller companies have sought alternative solutions, including parent company guarantees, letters of comfort, advance payments or separate bank accounts[89].

10.8   If the client is required to set up a trust account and pay into it at the beginning of each payment period the amount due for the next activity schedule or milestone, payment must be released at the appropriate time in an effective manner. The new approach set out in the NEC should lead the industry away from the process of monthly valuations and certification of interim payments. But if a contract does follow a Bill of Quantities route and monthly measurement, the employer, advised by the client's representative and/or professional quantity surveyor, must place an appropriate amount of money at the beginning of each month in the trust account. The sum allocated should correspond

---

[89] *I am particularly indebted to Ms Ann Minogue of McKenna & Co. for this information (see also her article in "Building" magazine on 25 February 1994) and for her helpful advice on this Chapter and others.*

---

to a pre-agreed programme. The contractor and the subcontractors should be advised by the client's representative of the amount so deposited. If any of them consider the sum to be inadequate, they should have a right to approach the adjudicator for a ruling on whether this sum should be increased. Failure to increase it after decision by the adjudicator should entitle an aggrieved participant to suspend the work (a right not usually available under existing main contract documentation[90]) until the sum in the trust account is increased.

10.9 I have considered whether the trust funds should make separate payments to the main contractor and to subcontractors, or even if there should be separate accounts. The subcontractors favour such a system. The SEACC[91] procurement system provides for main contractors and subcontractors to be identified separately. However, some clients may not be prepared to accept such a process, and may only be willing to set up one single trust account and make one payment out of it for each milestone/interim period. Whilst the subcontractors' concerns are understandable under the current system, they should no longer have reason to feel threatened in the future because:

1. Money must be deposited by the client in advance, at the beginning of each payment period. The client will also have been notified who the first line subcontractors are.

2. There is a suitably drawn up trust account, so they know that their payment will be safe even if the main contractor fails. Legislation will be needed to ensure that, in the event of the failure of the main contractor, trustees will have the duty of making due payments out of the trust account to subcontractors for work done and materials supplied. If the client fails, the trustees will pay the contractor, who will be contractually required to pay the subcontractors.

3. The contract and subcontract documents will involve a specific duty to trade fairly and to build up team work. New legislation relating to unfair terms will be introduced.

4. A comprehensive adjudication process will be in place, and the procedures relating to set off will have been regulated.

5. Clear and specific payment times will have been established and mandatory payment of interest if they are not honoured.

10.10 Although I do not feel able to recommend that subcontractors' payments should normally be made directly to them out of trust funds rather than through the main contractor (other than in cases of insolvency), some clients may wish to have this option. It would be possible for the model in the SEACC system to be incorporated as a special condition or option within the NEC or other Standard Forms. That would require discussions with the Electrical Contractors Association, as holders of the copyright of SEACC.

10.11 A suggestion made to the Review by the CIEC is that there should be a cut-off point in value of contract below which the trust fund arrangements should be unnecessary, either because the timescale of the contract is too short or the value of the work too low to justify it. (It suggested £¼ million.) Alternatively, certain classes of contract should be excluded, such as consumer contracts. While I can see the logic in such suggestions, I am doubtful about them. Any cut-off point runs the risk of the contract being divided into

---

[90] *Provision for suspension by the main contractor is available under MF/1 and MF/2, the IChemE "Red Book" and the ICE Design and Construct Conditions. Subcontractors have similar rights under DOM/1 and other standard forms of subcontract.*

[91] *I wish to record special thanks to Mr Giles Dixon of Turner Kenneth Brown for his helpful advice and briefing throughout the Review, and especially about the SEACC system and adjudication and conciliation/mediation procedures generally.*

small sections to avoid trust funds. But the amount of money involved in a small contract, though not great, may be very significant to those involved. If there are to be any exclusions at all I would suggest that they be limited to projects which are excluded from the CDM Regulations. Trust funds do not need to be set up for ordinary domestic work carried out without a formal contract document. Householders tend to pay for such work after it is completed in any case, or by stage payments informally agreed with the contractor.

10.12 Any interest accrued in the trust account should be entirely payable to the client. If the client wishes to make a charge to the contractor for the cost of operating a trust account, the charge should be agreed at tender stage and be included within the contract document. If necessary, a "cap" should be fixed to it, as in the German law. But it would be better if this could be resolved amicably between the parties in an atmosphere of cooperation. If the contractor decides to apportion some of the cost to the subcontractors, they should be told the cost which is being incurred by the contractor and how it is to be shared. It would be wrong for the contractor to seek to apportion the total cost to each of the subcontractors as, in effect, a "handling charge". If the main contractor wishes to impose some administration charge for passing on money to subcontractors, it should be explicitly identified as such in the contract documentation rather than being described as a "prompt payment discount". There is no longer any justification for such "discounts". Payment should be on time.

10.13 The introduction of a right of suspension of work in the main contract should not be limited to the failure of the employer to place money in the trust account. It should also be available if the employer fails to release it from the trust fund or if the architect or engineer fails to issue a payment certificate on time without good cause. However, suspension should only become available if the adjudicator has first been involved and has issued a decision, which the employer has then failed to honour with immediate effect.

10.14 These trust funds must also be mandatory for public sector clients. While main contractors expect to be paid by a public sector client, who is unlikely to become insolvent, such funds will be a crucial source of reassurance for subcontractors if the main contractor fails during the course of the job.

10.15 Some evidence to the Review has pressed strongly for a Builders Lien Act similar to that in the United States or some Provinces of Canada. This is a complex legislative procedure. I believe that mandatory trust accounts and the other safeguards set out in the report will provide protection for payment due to main and specialist contractors. A lien is a weak defence. Funders may have established prior charges on the property, which dilute the potential equity available to be released to other creditors in the event of a forced sale.

10.16 Some participants have pressed for wider reforms of the insolvency laws. In its final report, the CIEC advocates:

1. A statutory right of the contractor to information about the charges and other rights over the site and of the covenants in the funding agreement (as in all provinces in Canada except Newfoundland).

2. Failing such a right, an amendment to the Insolvency Act 1986 to deny any added value on site to a funder who has delayed terminating the funding agreement beyond the period when that funder knew that the client was in financial difficulties. The funder's fixed charge would lose its priority in such circumstances.

3. Alternatively, alteration to the law of retention of title so as to prevent the transfer of ownership of materials/goods already fixed in the project until payment has been made to the contractor (or else giving the contractor the right

to detach materials, where feasible). The Building Structures Group makes a similar recommendation.

10.17   I feel that these three proposals need further debate before a recommendation can be made. There will be time for the Implementation Forum to consider them while the Construction Contracts Bill is being drafted.

Recommendation 27: Trust Funds

10.18   I have already recommended that mandatory trust funds for payment should be established for construction work governed by formal conditions of contract (see Chapter 8). It is important that public sector clients have the same requirements, in order to maintain confidence amongst subcontractors. If the main contractor fails, it would be the duty of the trustee to ensure direct payment out of the trust fund to subcontractors. If the client fails, payments would be made out of the trust fund to the contractor. Similar arrangements should cover retention monies if that system continues (see Chapter 11). The statutory provisions should ensure that the trustees are legally empowered to make full payments direct to contractors or subcontractors for work done, or materials supplied and/or already incorporated within the work, without the Receiver of the failed participant being allowed to take such monies on behalf of other creditors[92] . Separate provisions will be required for Scottish Law, but I am told that it is possible to devise them to obtain the same results[93].

---

[92]   *The effect of this would be to overturn the British Eagle Judgement.*

[93]   *CIEC final report, quoting advice from a leading Scottish law firm.*

11.1 Defects should not be inevitable in a building or other form of construction project. The aim should be "right first time, every time". Some clients believe that the very concept of "practical completion" should be rejected, because the building is not complete so far as the client is concerned until all defects and snagging have been satisfactorily sorted out[94]. Customers who buy household consumer goods expect them to work. If they do not, they take them back to the shop. One cannot take back a building or refurbishment project. But clients are entitled to satisfaction at the end of the defects liability period. **The retention system is supposed to be a mechanism whereby clients can build up a fund during the course of a project which will act as an inducement to the contractor to remedy any defect during the liability period. The idea in principle is a sound one, though in practice the system no longer operates in that manner. A better option would be to replace it in the contracts with retention bonds[95], reducing in value as each milestone section of the work is completed. Some clients may prefer a cash retention system, and that option should also be available for them, provided that the money is retained in a secure trust fund.** It is not in dispute that the client needs some defence mechanism to ensure that the project is satisfactorily completed.

11.2 Difficult problems arise if the defects remain hidden ("latent") during the defects liability period and only emerge afterwards. Clients, and especially property developers seeking to let buildings on full repairing and insuring leases, need to be sure that there is no "black hole" of liability if significant defects arise later. Tenants will not be prepared to accept such leases without protection. Case law in recent years has closed the tort of negligence as a possible route for recovery of economic loss to the client, save in exceptional cases. The result has been the plethora of collateral warranties, which can involve those holding the warranties in uninsurable and possibly ruinous risks.

11.3 In addition to completion on time and within budget, and the attainment of reliable quality, clients and the industry need to know:

1. the responsibilities and rights of participants in construction projects should matters go awry; and

2. the prospects of adequate and timely restitution.

The current arrangements are inadequate.

---

[94] *It is surprising that there is no definition in the standard contract documents of what constitutes "practical completion". This matter should be addressed by the JCT. Subcontractors should also have the right to know when the architect has certified "practical completion". At the very least, a notice should be displayed on the building by the architect or some other appropriate notification procedures adopted.*

[95] *An argument used against retention bonds is that they might be much more expensive than retention, and might tempt the client's quantity surveyor to undervalue interim work as a precaution (CIEC final report). The former would presumably depend upon the reputation of the contractor, and the latter could be referred to an adjudicator, or be overcome by the use of milestones/activity schedules.*

11.4 There is widespread dissatisfaction with the present situation. It has generated a number of reports during the last 15 years of which the most significant are:

1. "Building Users Insurance Against Latent Defects" (known as the "BUILD Report", NEDC, 1988).

2. "Professional liability - report of the study teams", (known as the Likierman Report, HMSO, 1989).

3. Two European documents - the GAIPEC Report ("results of the work of the Group of European Inter Professional and Trade Associations for the building industry", September 1992) and the European Commission's "Staff Discussion Paper .... with Regard to Liabilities and Guarantees in the Construction Sector", June 1993.

Fault based restitution: post-acceptance law reform

11.5 Pursuit of rights by litigation is nearly always protracted and costly. Should negotiation fail, litigants decide whether the facts and their resources justify the risk implicit in court action.

11.6 Legal costs can mount rapidly. Counsel's opinions, experts' reports and discovery all contribute to diversion of management effort, as defences are probed to unravel uncertainties. These include:

1. Whether any or all of the claims are out-of-time;

2. challenging the facts, the existence of the alleged defect or damage and the cost of restitution;

3. throwing doubt on causes, of which there may be several;

4. challenging the degree of fault attributable to any participant.

11.7 Matters are also complicated by the number of parties joined in many actions. If one or more of the parties ceases to trade, the cost falls onto the others.

11.8 The upshot is unsatisfactory. Participants may be joined in actions with more regard to their assets and insurance cover than to their alleged culpability. Recovery of damage is risky and often long delayed.

11.9 In order to seek rationalisation of the law, a working party was set up last year chaired by a senior official of the DOE, comprising representatives of clients, contractors, consultants and specialist/trade contractors. At the date of finalising my Report, the working party had not reached complete agreement, although discussions were continuing. At that stage, the Constructors' Liaison Group were unable to accept some of the recommendations in the form which they were put forward.

1. **Joint Liability**

   i. The group recommended that in construction cases (other than personal injury), defendants should have their liability limited to a fair proportion of the plaintiff's loss, having regard to the relative degree of blame. Defendants who are only liable for some of the latent damage should not have to suffer 100% liability because other defendants are unable or unwilling to bear their share of the loss.

    ii.   The CLG agreed with this recommendation.

2. Limitation (Prescription) Periods

    i.   The majority of the group recommended that a single period of 10 years of limitation (prescription in Scotland) should be fixed from the date of practical completion or effective occupation. This should apply for breaches of contract, whether or not under seal (or their equivalents in Scotland) or for negligent actions in tort (delict in Scotland).

    ii.   The CLG rejected this recommendation, because it referred to the practical completion of the main contract, whereas the specialists' work might have been finished years earlier, and the new ten year period would in practice extend their liabilities. CLG believed that a project based system would be unfair to specialists. The limitation period should begin when they have completed their subcontract work. Alternatively, the limitation period for engineering services should be shortened to 5 years, as happens in some European countries.

3. Transfer of Clients' Rights

    i.   The majority of the group recommended that if all or any part of a project is legally transferred by a client to an owner (or from an owner to a successive owner or from the client or an owner to a tenant with a full repairing and insuring lease or paying these costs by way of a full service charge), the client's contractual rights should automatically be made available to all or any such successive owner or owners and/or tenant or tenants of all or any part of the project. There were 3 exceptions:

        a.   Damage to moveable "other" property.

        b.   Damage to the personal property of the occupants.

        c.   Any losses other than the cost of repair and reinstatement of the project. This would acknowledge that consequential and economic loss by subsequent owners or tenants cannot be the responsibility of the construction team except where it relates directly to the repair and reinstatement of the building to its originally intended condition, with the damage eliminated.

    ii.   The CLG felt that these recommendations went too far and were unlikely to be insurable. They believed that:

        a.   Tenants' rights of action should be via the current owner.

        b.   The right should be for the repair of the building only, and not involve any economic or consequential loss.

        c.   Payments should properly have been discharged when due under the contract and rights of action should be reciprocal so that other specialists have equivalent rights of action against clients and their advisers.

4. Consumer Protection

The majority report wanted substantial implementation of the 1988 "Beat the Cowboys" report[96]. The CLG argued that events had moved on since then and in any case aspects of that report (such as low cost arbitration and Codes of Practice supported by the Office of Fair Trading) were inadequate or had proved unachievable in practice.

11.10   I do not comment further on paragraph 11.9(4) because, as the Interim Report made clear, small domestic jobs dealt with under the "Beat the Cowboys" report are largely outside my terms of reference. They rarely involve formal Standard Contract documents. Procurement issues are not a major problem either. The proposals for quality registration may assist indirectly in raising standards in the domestic field.[97]

11.11   So far as the other 3 sets of recommendations of the working group are concerned, I believe they should be accepted and implemented, because:-

1. The working group's package is intended to be a total one. The exclusion of joint liability means that no party would pay for more than their adjudged contribution to the cause of the damage. That is a totally different approach to the current arrangements of collateral warranties (some of them very onerous) with litigants seeking to pursue defendants with the "deepest pockets", leading to expensive and very lengthy multiparty actions. Other members of the working group are unhappy about some aspects of the proposals, but have accepted the overall package as a fair one. The BPF have made it clear that they would regard a reduction of the specialist/trade contractors' liability period to 5 years as unacceptable, and they also reject the proposal that the periods of liability should begin when subcontractors complete their particular sections of the work (source: Letter from the BPF, May 1994).

2. Some of the concerns of the specialist/trade contractors arise from other conditions of trading or unhappy experiences between themselves and main contractors. I have made detailed recommendations about such matters in other parts of this report, to obtain more acceptable arrangements.

3. A still wider package may well be necessary in any case, involving compulsory "BUILD" insurance.

11.12   The working group's recommendations would require new legislation. As with the 1972 Defective Premises Act, it would ignore the contractual arrangements which can lead to injustice and lack of remedy for the client if the contractor has failed or gone away, and the defective work was in any case carried out by a subcontractor. It would allow the client to identify the responsible party and take action, whether or not they were originally in contract with each other. That can only be achieved at present if there is a collateral warranty and if such a warranty is in practice enforceable.

---

[96] *Report of the "Beat the Cowboys" working party, HMSO, 1988.*

[97]   *As part of their comments on dispute resolution, the Building Structures Group, in their final recommendations, suggested that a new system should be set up for very small contracts between a householder and a builder. They recommended that a construction regulator, appointed by the DOE, should name regional referees to settle such disputes, but only if the householder had entered into a Standard Contract with a registered builder. I would respond that if a Standard Contract such as the Minor Works Form is used, there ought to be an adjudication, conciliation or mediation procedure within it. However, if the householder is proceeding on the basis of a personal meeting with the builder, a written estimate or an exchange of letters, I believe that such work falls outside the scope of this Review.*

11.13 Lawyers who are expert in this field have advised me that if the working group's proposed change in the law was enacted, it would remove the requirement for many collateral warranties. That would be welcome. But it would still not be certain that clients could obtain the financial outcome they seek, especially if those found responsible for defects were under-insured or no longer trading.

Suppliers' Liability

11.14 I have received evidence from the CIEC (and others) about the liability of firms supplying goods and materials to main and specialist/trade contractors. In its final report, the CIEC suggests that the suppliers' ability to contract out of their liability by exclusion clauses should be restricted. (The National Council of Building Materials Producers (BMP), who are members of the CIEC, disassociated themselves from this recommendation.) There does appear to be a disparity between suppliers' liability and those of the others in the construction chain. However, this touches on wider issues relating to sale of goods legislation. I do not feel that there has been sufficient evidence or discussion of this specific problem for me to make any recommendation. However, it could be discussed further by the proposed Implementation Forum.

Recommendation 28: Liability Legislation

11.15 I recommend that the Construction Contracts Bill should include provisions to implement the majority report of the working party on liability. Corresponding legislative provisions should be introduced for Scotland.

Restitution as of right: first party material damage insurance

11.16 A right to sue does not amount to a right of restitution. It still requires litigation. Reliable and timely restitution has been shown to result only from first party material damage non-cancellable insurance[98]. Within the terms of the policy, repairs are funded on proof of relevant damage, without proof of fault. Such arrangements may be statutory or discretionary. An advantage of a statutory system is that it can provide a clear framework for the rights and responsibilities of the industry and clients.

11.17 Some insurance provision is already available within the United Kingdom[99]. The Joint Contracts Tribunal is in the process of drafting its own latent defects insurance policy.

---

[98] *See the "BUILD report" op cit and "Restitution for Latent Defects: There must be a better way" paper by Professor Donald Bishop to the Barbican conference, December 1993, to be published by the CIC. I am grateful to Professor Bishop for his guidance on this section of the Report, and some others.*

[99] *For example, Griffiths & Armour offer "Bild", operated with General Accident and Commercial Union, which also involves automatic waiving of subrogation rights, except of suppliers. To achieve waiving of subrogation, the projects must have engineers who are members of the Association of Consulting Engineers working on them.*

The Association of British Insurers told the Review that latent defects insurance has not been a strong feature of the market so far in Britain through lack of demand. If, however, the market improved and demand strengthened, it would be possible to provide ten year latent defects cover and thereby obviate the need for widespread collateral warranties.

11.18   There are two ways by which latent defects insurance can be made widely available in the form of restitution as of right. They are:

1.   To adopt the French decennial guarantee system (as in the Loi Spinetta 1978, as amended in 1983). This is a statutory system linked to the Code Napoleon, and cannot be set aside by contract. It does, however, involve strict liability on all producers of building projects unless they can show that the damage was beyond their control. Liability is for damage discovered within 10 years of acceptance which "affects the solidity of access roads, main conduits, foundations, structural elements, enclosing or covering works and fixed equipment"; or "which renders the works unfit for their intended use". Timely restitution in France involves clients, except for exempted bodies in the public sector, taking out compulsory "Dommage Ouvrage" cover, which is project based and automatically assigned to future owners. It provides a fund to carry out damage repair without seeking to establish liability and without any provision for excess. Producers are required to insure their decennial liability. That responsibility falls upon contractors, professionals and manufacturers or suppliers of components, or any one else bound by contract to the client, but not subcontractors. Both sets of insurances are for the entire statutory liability. Litigation is avoided in practice by a concordat apportioning responsibility for payment between the insurers. Only about 10 cases a year now go to court. About 85% of cases are settled within 20 working weeks. The cost of insurance has fallen sharply, having originally been high. The estimated aggregate cost of it, as apportioned between the client and construction team, is about 3.5% of the total cost of the project.

2.   "BUILD" insurance for non-domestic clients. This is either financed by the client (currently about 1% of construction cost) or with the cost shared/ apportioned between the principal participants such as clients, lead consultants and contractors (who might then require their main subcontractors to contribute) and which is recommended to exclude rights of subrogation. Such policies were originally intended to cover the structure, including foundations and weather shield envelope. They do not normally cover engineering services, which is regarded by clients as a serious weakness. It is however possible to insure separately against M&E failure for between 1 and 5 years. "BUILD" policies can also involve cover for loss of rental income or additional rental expenditure.

11.19   Since clients can already obtain "BUILD" insurance if they so wish, it might asked why it should be thought necessary to stimulate demand. The introduction of mandatory insurance would be a logical extension to the recommendations of the Liability Working Party, which themselves require legislation. If the insurance companies were to become significant players in construction quality and standards (as opposed to all-risks or other site based insurance which they currently cover as part of the Standard Forms of Contract), they would insist upon their own involvement in supervision[100]. In France, technical inspectors or technical control bureaux are employed by clients to check drawings at various stages and inspect the work on site. Such supervision by client's representatives often results in a discount on the insurance premium. The technical inspectors are an

---

[100] *For example "Bild" involves a compulsory technical audit before cover is arranged. (Source: article by Mr Philip Robinson of Griffiths and Armour, "Latent Defects and Existing Buildings", Financial Times "World Policy Guide", March 1994.)*

officially recognised profession, independent of the insurance companies and are widely believed to have helped to raise standards of construction in France. Some such inspectors are also employed by contractors as safety or quality consultants. (This is a possible new role for Approved Inspectors in Britain, or other suitably qualified technical experts.)

11.20   Another benefit of substantial involvement by the insurance companies would be to extend knowledge of defects and how to rectify them. The Construction Quality Forum, launched last November by the Building Research Establishment in conjunction with some representatives of the industry, clients and professions, aims to provide systematic feed back on building problems and draw up a defects data base. However, the equivalent organisation in France, the AQC, is financed by a levy on insurance premia. It collects information on defects and issues advice and guidance notes accordingly. An insurance system in Britain could provide significant additional funding for a research, development and information service by an addition to insurance premia, payable to such an agency (see also Chapter 7, paragraphs 7.39 to 7.40).

11.21   While this will take time to achieve, an agency might become capable of running the registers based on CMIS and ConReg. Insurers who are taking risks on quality will undoubtedly wish to satisfy themselves of the standards of performance of the consultants, contractors and subcontractors whose work they are insuring. They might develop a "Star" system, with premia linked to the standard of the firms concerned. Some firms may find it difficult to get insurance or, if the client is paying for the cover, to get work on projects paid for by the client. If that restricted the activities of poor performers, clients and the industry as a whole could only benefit.

11.22   Such insurance should be limited to specific building projects. It is not required in civil engineering in France (though the engineer is normally insured), and there is no obvious need to extend it to civil engineering or process engineering in the United Kingdom[101]. The insurance industry has indicated that it would welcome a mandatory contractual requirement for defects liability insurance, but does not, in principle, support statutory requirements.

11.23   The French dual system of compulsory producers' decennial insurance and clients' damage insurance is an attractive option, but is too large a step. It would seem reasonable at this stage to bring within the mandatory insurance system all new commercial, retail and industrial building work, subject to a de minimis cut off point in value,[102] including work for public sector clients such as offices or industrial premises. The basis of the requirement should be as set out for "BUILD" insurance in paragraph 11.18(2) above. This should be discussed with the insurance industry to establish, inter alia, the appropriate timescale for its introduction.

---

[101] *However, the CIPS final report does recommend compulsory decennial insurance for civil engineering work, but not if the works are in the public sector.*

[102] *British latent defect insurance tends to have an excess provision.*

11.24

1. The Construction Contracts Bill should contain a provision for compulsory latent defects insurance for 10 years from practical completion for all future new commercial, retail and industrial building work (including any such public sector schemes), with a minimum value cut off point which would be subject to periodic review in the light of movement of building costs.

2. The basis of the insurance should be as defined in paragraph 11.18(2), but with cover for rental income loss/additional rental expenditure only as a voluntary clause for the client. (More comprehensive cover could be negotiated.)

3. The policy should require the cost of the premium to be shared amongst the principal participants in the project, and exclude subrogation.

4. It would be possible to eliminate any excess, if the participants are prepared to pay extra, but this should not be a statutory requirement.

5. The date of introduction of the new provision should allow proper time for future projects to be priced to take account of this additional cost and for the insurance market to prepare for its introduction.

6. If it were to appear that such legislation might be delayed, the organisations responsible for contract conditions (including Government Departments) should consider inserting such a clause or clauses as a contractual requirement within existing forms of contract for building work, including the New Engineering Contract.

7. The insurance companies, in conjunction with clients and the industry, should set up a Quality Bureau, perhaps based on the Construction Quality Forum, with a levy to fund it through an addition to the insurance premium. The levy should be used for research and information feedback, to raise quality standards and site performance.

12.1   The Review has come to an end with the publication of the Final Report. It is for Ministers and the parties to the Review to decide what, if any, action they wish to take to implement its recommendations. However, as I indicated in Chapter 1 of this Report, the "chemistry" and mutual understanding achieved in the Assessors' meetings, and in the back-up which has supported them, has been remarkable. It would be a pity if it were now to be ended and the valuable understanding dispersed. The involvement of all participants around the table has been essential for this Review. The total commitment to it by the two client organisations has been particularly significant.

12.2   Encouragingly, the participating organisations wish to keep the momentum going in different ways, as do others. For example:-

1. **The CIPS**

    The Chartered Institute attaches great importance to early implementation. Its report recommends a two-tier structure:-

    a.   A Standing Strategic Group for the Construction Industries, chaired by the Minister for Construction, to meet twice a year to review progress in implementing the Report.

    b.   The creation of a Government/client/industry organisation called Construction Sourcing Ltd for the purpose of implementing it.

    Its proposals are reproduced as Appendix VI.

2. **The CIC**

    The Council wishes to continue the high level forum of monthly meetings, without any break in continuity. It says that the successor forum must be supported by the CIC, CIEC and CLG at the highest level, and must continue to involve clients. It must have fundamental support (and funding) from the Government. While the CIC does not comment on the proposal of one of its member organisations (CIOB) for a Construction Industry Development Board, it stresses that any such organisation should be 70% funded by Government, be project based and with the lowest possible level of bureaucracy.

3. **The CIEC**

    The Council does not want the momentum to be lost. It wishes the Assessors, or other individuals nominated by the bodies which they represent, to meet on a monthly basis until the end of 1994, and thereby identify and carry forward those proposals which require concerted industry action. It does not favour any large or bureaucratic regulatory structure. While it basically believes that any recommendations can be implemented within the existing industry representative bodies, it points out that if the Assessors felt that a new body was necessary by the end of 1994, it could be set up at that stage.

4. **The NSCC**

The Council's final report does not suggest any implementation mechanisms, but makes 11 recommendations, some of which would require legislation.

5. **The SECG**

The SECG favours the establishment of a new regulatory authority for the construction industry called OFCON (Office for Regulation of Construction). It would operate under a Construction Industry Charter, and have three arms. The first would be a National Registration Authority, which would accredit industry bodies concerned with national registration schemes. The Contracts Division would oversee procurement systems and conditions of contract, but the JCT would continue to produce standard documentation which conformed with the Charter. The third arm would be a Practice and Standards Division, which would monitor the work of the NJCC and ensure that it followed the procedures of the Charter. There would also be an Ombudsman, whose staff would be independent of OFCON, and who would have statutory powers to regulate the three divisions and deal with any deviations from good practice, including fines or deregistration of an "habitual offender". The SECG does not believe that voluntary arrangements will prove effective.

6. **The BPF**

The BPF's final report does not specify any actual implementation mechanisms, but it makes 21 recommendations for action, many of which are also contained in this Report. The BPF has always stressed the crucial role of the client at the core of the construction process.

7. **The CIOB**

The Chartered Institute of Building is a member of the CIC. It favours the Assessors carrying on as an implementation group until a Construction Industry Development Board can be formed. The Board would be set up by the Government but run and funded by the industry. It should have minimum staffing and be a facilitating body designed to improve competitiveness and standards, develop market opportunities and improve market intelligence.

8. **The Building Structures Group**

The BSG is part of the Constructors Liaison Group. It favours the creation of a Construction Regulator as an Executive Agency of the DOE. The proposed Agency would have four main subsidiaries - a National Disputes Resolution Service, a Standard Contracts Service to take over the role of the JCT, a Good Practice Service to replace the NJCC and a Construction Registration Authority. The body would be statutory.

9. **The Ground Forum**

The Forum, which is a member of the CIC, favours the establishment of an Ombudsman for the industry to monitor compliance with a Code of Good Practice, with the ultimate power to suspend the right of firms to prequalify for public works until their record of observing the Code improves.

10. **The Association of Project Managers**

The APM recommends that a "single body" be set up to represent promoters and all participants in the construction industry, to issue a Code of Practice, monitor progress, and report to Government and industry.

11.   **Mr Robin Wilson**

Mr Wilson, who is the new chairman of the CIC, favours a Construction Industry Board, to be client led and chaired by a client or other eminent person. Its membership should be clients 4, DOE and DTI as regulators 2, CIC 2, CIEC 1, CLG 1. It should be concerned with promoting best practice, co-ordinating co-operative efforts such as contracts, research and private finance and be a forum for resolving current issues through consensus or convergence of views.

The Australian Experience

12.3   Some have drawn attention to the Construction Industry Development Association of Australia. This body was set up under the Construction Industry Reform and Development Act of 1992. Its task is to implement the Construction Industry In-Principle Reform and Development Agreement (IPA), which was signed by the Federal Government, several State Governments, Industry Associations, including clients and occupiers and Trade Unions. The Association has a fixed life, and will run until June 1995. Its budget is A$10 million (£5 million), 30% of which comes from industry. Its Mission Statement involves a commitment to bring about "real and measured change" and to "provide leadership, motivation and foster the development of increased capabilities". It has put forward a number of Codes of Practice - including prequalification criteria - and established Model Projects on which new approaches are trialled and monitored. It regards itself as having largely completed the task of identifying and developing the management tools and codes necessary to make significant changes. The priority now is implementation, and the intention in the Mission Statement is that the change process will become self-sustaining and extend beyond the life of the Association.

Recommendation 30: Possible Delivery Mechanisms

12.4   Delivery mechanisms imply that there is consensus on the way forward. I cannot assume that before the Report is even published! I recommend a step-by-step approach:-

1. **A Standing Strategic Group of the Construction Industry** should meet twice a year, chaired by the Secretary of State or another DOE Minister. Its membership should be drawn from the Presidents (Chairpersons), Chief Executives and possibly one other representative of: the Construction Clients' Forum; the CIC; the CIEC; and the CLG. It need not be concerned solely with the Review. It can also be the principal Forum for bringing clients and the industry together with Ministers to discuss matters of interest and importance relating to construction. A similar consultation body already exists, but client representation should be added to it.

2. **An Implementation Forum** should be set up, consisting of 1 or 2 Assessor representatives from each of the organisations on the Standing Strategic Group and the DOE, under a neutral chairperson. Between its first meeting (hopefully within a short period after publication of this Report) and the end of 1994, it should seek to advise the Standing Strategic Group:-

    a. which of the recommendations it believes can be implemented by existing agencies without any additional structures;

b.   on the timescale for drafting and introducing the Construction Strategy Code of Practice, the Construction Contracts Bill, registration, the new arrangements for selection of consultants and the restructuring of contract conditions;

c.   whether it favours the formal setting up of an Agency similar to that in Australia and, if so, under what format;

d.   whether or not it favours the appointment of an Ombudsman, to examine allegations of poor practice and issue public comments upon them. If the Ombudsman is to have any specific regulatory powers, as SECG, the BSG and the Ground Forum all favour, they will have to be statutorily defined if they are to be effective.

12.5 My own view is that any Agency should be concerned with offering leadership, co-ordinating the production of Codes, guidance and advice, and setting specific targets for progress. It should be kept extremely small, with a tight timescale of work of five years, to seek to deliver the proposed cost reduction programme between now and the end of the century. The "Construction Sourcing" proposals of the CIPS present a possible model. The Implementation Forum may wish to consider before the end of 1994 which of those proposals are most likely to be effective in achieving the results. If the concept of an agency is accepted, a business plan should be drawn up as quickly as possible. The various participants would need to share the costs, but I hope that the DOE would make a significant contribution.

12.6 I would not at this stage favour the appointment of an Ombudsman if there were also to be an Agency. The purpose of the Agency would be to encourage the delivery of best practice and performance, and to develop teamwork, rather than to judge alleged perpetrators of poor practice. Because it would involve client representation, an Agency would have much more authority throughout the entire construction process than the NJCC, which could be allowed to lapse. The recommendations in the Report relating to contract conditions and the Construction Contracts Bill should provide the necessary framework for progress without external policing. But the need for an Ombudsman should be kept under review by the Implementation Forum. The Forum itself should remain in existence until the implementation programme is clearly on course, or, if an Agency is to be formed, until it is fully launched.

12.7 The groups of recommendations which I have made fall into a number of categories. It will be for the implementation machinery to assess its own priorities, subject to the decisions of Ministers, but my recommendations for timescales are as follows:-

Task	Action by	Timescale
1. DOE designated as lead Department	Ministers	For both 1 & 2, urgent, but a matter for Ministers collectively. Hopefully
2. Government to commit itself to being a Best Practice Client	Ministers	before the end of summer recess.
3. Creation of Construction Clients' Forum	Client bodies, BPF, CIPS, ECI, and Construction Round Table	Urgent and before first meeting of Implementation Forum.
4. Check-list Guide on Briefing issued	CIC	6 months.

Task	Action by	Timescale
5. Construction Strategy Code of Practice dealing with Project and Contract Strategy, Project Management, selection of consultants and tendering procedures	DOE, in conjunction with Implementation Forum	Published as a draft for consultation in 8 months. Final version in 12 months.
6. Joint Code of Practice for Selection of Subcontractors	CIEC/CLG	To work in parallel with task 5, and publish within 4 months of it.
7. Involvement of Process Plant Clients in DOE discussions	DOE	As soon as possible.
8. Restructuring of JCT/CCSJC	Parties to those bodies and proposed new members	6 months.
9. Preparation of full matrix of documents by JCT/CCSJC, including CPI and signing off arrangements. Check list for all design work.	JCT/CCSJC, following reorganisation in conjunction with ICE	12 months after reorganisation.
10. Use of the NEC to increase	Client bodies including DOE, in conjunction with other Departments	As soon as possible.
11. Phasing out of GC/Works/1 and other Government Contract Conditions	DOE, and other Departments	3-4 years, pending evaluation of experience with NEC.
12. Working Party on quality/price selection of consultants	DOE, clients and CIC	6 months. Recommendations to be in draft of Code of Practice (see 5 above).
13. Expansion of ConReg	DOE, following consultation with CIC and clients	12 months.
14. Expansion of CMIS	DOE task force involving consultation with clients, CIEC and CLG	12-18 months, (progress of the EU scheme may have a bearing).
15. Examination of JAGNET report and further CIEC proposals	Appropriate Government departments, in conjunction with CITB and CIEC/CLG	12 months.
16. Task Force on image of industry	CIEC/CLG	3 months.

Task	Action by	Timescale
17. Co-ordinated Equal Opportunities Action Plans	CIC, CIEC and CLG	12 months.
18. Professional Education Task Force	CIC, with advice from clients and CIEC/CLG and Government Departments	12 months.
19. Decisions on Working Party on Liability proposals, BUILD Insurance and Research Levy	DOE, Assn of British Insurers, and all in the implementation Forum	6 months to formulate brief to Parliamentary Draftsmen for inclusion in Construction Contracts Bill.
20. Productivity Initiative	Strategy Group/ Ministers	Announcement as soon as possible. 5 year timescale for implementation.
21. Drafting of Construction Contracts Bill	DOE, in conjunction with Implementation Forum	12 months to draft. Bill to be presented to Parliament in 1995/6 session. Royal Assent, subject to Parliamentary approval, by July 1996. Implementation as from appointed days for different sections.
22. Formulation of recommendations on a possible Development Agency along the lines of the Construction Sourcing proposal	Implementation Forum, to advise the Strategy Group/Ministers	Advice in principle by January 1995. If affirmative, draft business plan by April 1995.

Conclusion

12.8 These tasks are substantial. The timescales are demanding. But the goodwill which has been evident throughout the Review encourages me to believe that they can be achieved. This great industry meets new challenges every day. I am sure that it can, and will, meet these as well.

To consider:

- current procurement and contractual arrangements; and

- current roles, responsibilities and performance of the participants, including the client.

with particular regard to:

- the processes by which clients' requirements are established and presented;

- methods of procurement;

- responsibility for the production, management and development of design;

- organisation and management of the construction processes;

- contractual issues and methods of dispute resolution; and

in doing so to take into account:

- the structure of the industry;

- the importance of fair and transparent competition;

- the desirability of a fair balance between the interests of, and the risks borne by, the client and the various parties involved in a project;

- the requirements of public accountability, value for money and EC legislation as regards public sector contracts;

- the importance of encouraging enterprise, the development of a skilled labour force and investment in improving quality and efficiency;

- current developments in law;

- relevant comparisons with the structure and performance of the construction industry in other countries;

with the objectives of making recommendations to Government, the construction industry and its clients regarding reform to reduce conflict and litigation and encourage the industry's productivity and competitiveness.

The detailed make up of the four funding bodies (other than the Department of the Environment) is as follows:-

Construction Industry Council

27 full members:-

Architects and Surveyors Institute, Association of Building Engineers, Association of Consultant Architects, Association of Consulting Engineers, Board of Incorporated Engineers and Technicians (ICE), British Flat Roofing Council, British Institute of Architectural Technologists, Building Services Research and Information Association, Chartered Institute of Building, Chartered Institute of Building Services Engineers, Construction Industry Research and Information Association, Consultant Quantity Surveyors Association, Ground Forum, Institute of Building Control, Institute of Construction Management, Institute of Clerks of Works of Great Britain, Institute of Highways Incorporated Engineers, Institute of Maintenance and Building Management, Institute of Plumbing, Institution of Civil Engineers, Institution of Civil Engineering Surveyors, Institution of Structural Engineers, Landscape Institute, Royal Institute of British Architects, Royal Institution of Chartered Surveyors, Royal Town Planning Institute, Society of Surveying Technicians.

10 associate members:-

Association of Heads of Surveying, Building Centre Trust, Building Research Establishment, Construction Industry Computing Association, Construction Industry Training Board (Northern Ireland), District Surveyors Association, Faculty of Building, Institute of Concrete Technology, Royal Incorporation of Architects in Scotland, Standing Conference of Heads of Schools of Architecture.

Construction Industry Employers Council

The Building Employers Confederation

The Federation of Civil Engineering Contractors

The Federation of Master Builders

The National Council of Building Materials Producers

The National Specialist Contractors Council (which is involved separately in the Review as a funding body in its own right).

National Specialist Contractors Council

The Federation of Associations of Specialists and Sub-Contractors

The Federation of Building Specialist Contractors

(Both these organisations contain individual member Federations and Associations, currently 18 in total.)

Specialist Engineering Contractors' Group

The Electrical Contractors Association

The Electrical Contractors Association of Scotland

The Heating and Ventilating Contractors Association

The National Association of Lift Makers

The National Association of Plumbing, Heating and Mechanical Services Contractors

NB

In October 1993 the NSCC and the SECG came together with the Building Structures Group (itself a new organisation of 7 Federations/ Associations) to form the Constructors Liaison Group as a reference and liaison centre for matters affecting the common interests of their member trade associations. All these Associations and the Groups continue to operate separately. As the Report went to press, it was announced that the BEC and FCEC, supported by major construction firms, had commissioned a study by consultants about the possible formation of a new construction employers' organisation provisionally to be called "Newco".

First phase (before 13 December 1993)

1.   "Building" Editorial Advisory Panel
2.   Peter Thurnham, MP
3.   Department of the Environment (DOE) and Central Unit on Procurement (CUP)
4.   Ian Dixon, CBE (CIC assessor)
5.   Martin Barnes, Coopers and Lybrand
6.   Stephen Davies, Building Employers Confederation (BEC) and Philip Povey, Joint Secretary, Joint Contracts Tribunal (JCT)
7.   Assessors' meeting
8.   Federation of Civil Engineering Contractors
9.   Frank Griffiths, Monty Burton and Peter Marsh (CIPS assessor and team)
10.   Davis Langdon Everest
11.   Chris Sneath (SECG assessor)
12.   Antony Carr (NSCC assessor)
13.   Ian Dixon, CBE and Graham Watts (CIC)
14.   David Anderson (CIEC assessor)
15.   Will McKee (BPF assessor)
16.   David Anderson
17.   Construction Round Table
18.   Scarlett Burkett Griffiths
19.   Stefan Tietz
20.   Burrell, Hayward and Budd
21.   Austin-Smith: Lord
22.   Troup Bywaters & Anders
23.   Ove Arup
24.   Watts & Partners
25.   Giles Dixon, Turner Kenneth Brown
26.   National Joint Consultative Committee
27.   BEC and Federation of Master Builders (FMB)
28.   Assessors' meeting
29.   Electrical Contractors Association (ECA) and Giles Dixon
30.   James R Knowles Claims Conference
31.   Colonel J Weir, Jeakins Weir Ltd
32.   SJ Farmer (Long Eaton)
33.   President's Consultative Committee (BEC)
34.   BPF Review back-up panel
35.   JCT - Chairman and Joint Secretaries
36.   Giffen Group

[103] *The meetings are listed in chronological order.*

37. Peter Rogers, Stanhope
38. Royal Institute of British Architects
39. ECA
40. NSCC back up team
41. Assessors' meeting
42. Institution of Civil Engineers
43. John Sims
44. CIPS seminar
45. Launch of Constructors Liaison Group
46. Giles Dixon
47. David Anderson
48. Graham Watts
49. Ann Minogue, McKenna & Co
50. Royal Incorporation of Architects in Scotland
51. Scottish Building Contract Committee
52. Scottish Office
53. BEC annual conference
54. "Profit from Innovation" launch, CIC
55. British Association of Landscape Industries
56. Building Research Establishment Construction Quality Forum launch
57. Innovation Policy Research Associates
58. Assessors' meeting

Second phase (after 13 December 1993)

1. Ian Dixon, CBE
2. David Anderson
3. Antony Carr
4. Chris Sneath
5. Will McKee
6. Frank Griffiths
7. Stephen Porter, British Airways
8. Assessors' meeting
9. MACE
10. Bernard Rimmer, Slough Estates
11. Construction Industry Research and Information Association
12. Building Structures Group
13. Association of Consulting Engineers (ACE)
14. Stent Foundations Ltd
15. Sir Peter Levene, George Iacobiescu (Canary Wharf) Malcolm Hutchinson, Stephen Gibbs, Reg Woodman (Docklands Light Railway)
16. Centre for Dispute Resolution (CEDR), ADR Group, British Academy of Experts, Chartered Institute of Arbitrators.
17. DOE and Gardiner Theobold Management Services
18. Peter Thurnham, MP
19. Chartered Institute of Building Services Engineers (CIBSE)
20. Scottish Joint Consultative Committee & Scottish Construction Industry Group
21. Reading University

22. Electrical Contractors Association
23. All Party Construction group, Houses of Parliament
24. Assessors' meeting
25. Tony Baldry MP
26. Len Bunton, Muirheads Beard Dove
27. Tony Bingham
28. Health and Safety Executive
29. Derek Hammond
30. CUP
31. Construction Employers' Federation (Northern Ireland)
32. Northern Ireland Government Departments
33. Royal Society of Ulster Architects, Royal Institution of Chartered Surveyors (Northern Ireland) and ACE (Northern Ireland)
34. Confederation of Associations of Specialist Engineering Contractors (Northern Ireland)
35. Jim Burgess
36. DTI Small Firms Unit
37. Antony Carr
38. Institute of Roofing
39. Department of Transport
40. Construction Round Table
41. Stephen Moon, BEC
42. Chartered Institute of Building
43. Confederation of Construction Specialists
44. British Constructional Steelwork Association (BCSA)
45. Association of British Insurers
46. Sir Brian Hill and Jennie Price (BEC)
47. Official Referees' Solicitors Association
48. Ministry of Defence
49. Arnold Project Services
50. JCT - Chairman and Joint Secretaries
51. National Audit Office
52. National Contractors Group
53. Sir Andrew Derbyshire and Graham Watts
54. Institute of Plumbing
55. CIBSE conference
56. Association of Project Managers
57. Masons
58. CIEC steering group
59. Donald Bishop
60. Junior Liaison Organisation
61. European Construction Institute
62. BEC and FMB
63. Paul Hodgkinson, Simons Group
64. Colin Andrews, Bovis
65. Keith Allsop
66. BEC

67. Peter Jordan, Building Projects Information Committee.

68. Chartered Institute of Arbitrators

69. Kier Group

70. Ove Arup

71. SECG steering group

72. Assessors' meeting

73. DOE

74. Ken Dixon, Sylvester Bone, Sandy Mackay and Graham Watts

75. David Anderson and Jennie Price

76. CIPS conference

77. DTI (Consumer Affairs Division)

78. BCSA

79. GEM

80. Assessors' meeting

81. Sir George Young MP

82. John Gains, Mowlems

83. Martin Barnes, Coopers and Lybrand

84. Lawrence Haines, Highways Agency

85. The Major Contractors' Group

There were also many informal contacts on the telephone and at industry functions, some of which Sir Michael addressed.

JCT

1. The existing membership of the Joint Contracts Tribunal is as follows:-

Professional Bodies	Clients	Main Contractors	Specialist/Trade (Sub) Contractors	Others
RIBA - 4	BPF -3	BEC - 6*	CASEC - 2	SBCC - 2
RICS - 4	LAAs - 10		FASS- 2	
ACE- 2				

*   *BEC gives two of its seats to subcontractors who are in the membership of the FBSC.*

\+   *DOE and NHS Estates have 1 observer each.*

2. There are, in practice four main participants within the contracting process. They are clients, professional consultants, main contractors and specialist/trade (sub) contractors. The JCT has no direct representation of private sector clients other than property developers, and its public sector members all represent local authorities. It does not provide for contracts/agreements between clients and consultants, nor between main contractors and subcontractors, unless they are nominated or, in limited cases, "named". There is therefore no total matrix of documentation available to the client. The representation on the JCT of the organisations does not reflect the modern structure of the industry, whereby the professional organisations gather together under the Construction Industry Council, the main contractors (and some subcontractors) under the Construction Industry Employers Council and the specialists under the Constructors Liaison Group. The presence of the Scottish Building Contract Committee (SBCC) as full members is somewhat anomalous, since it has its own Committee and Scottish contract documents.

3. A restructured JCT should take the following form:-

    1. The Construction Clients' Forum should nominate 9 private sector members. Clearly it would be sensible if its representation came from as wide a spectrum as possible.

    2. The public sector clients should also have nine seats, of which four should be for the Local Authority Associations and the remainder divided between Government procurers and significant public sector agency clients, including the housing association movement. The Department of the Environment should take responsibility for allocating such seats, and keeping the distribution of them under review.

3. The CIC, the CIEC and the CLG should each have nine seats, to be distributed amongst their members as they judge best.

4. The SBCC should retain observer status if it so wishes, and may wish to consider its own structure, to reflect changes in the JCT.

4. The membership should be grouped into a series of four "colleges" - clients (public and private), consultants (CIC), main contractors (CIEC) and specialist/trade (sub) contractors (CLG).

5. In order to create a complete family of interlocking documents, in accordance with the principles of Chapter 5.18, there should be a series of sub-committees. Thus:-

1. A sub-committee of clients and the CIC should be responsible for preparing a matrix of consultants' conditions of engagement, interlocking with each other and with the main building contracts.

2. A sub-committee of clients and the CIEC should prepare main contract documents.

3. A sub-committee of the CIEC and the CLG should prepare domestic subcontract documents.

4. A sub-committee of clients, the CIEC and the CLG should prepare nominated or "named" subcontract documents, if these are still desired.

As the New Engineering Contract already incorporates many of the principles of Chapter 5.18, it would be best if it were used as the basis for the work of the committees. The ICE would have to be involved as it holds the copyright.

6. Equal representation of both (or all, in the case of 5(4)) parties should be permitted on the sub-committees. Other parties should be invited to attend and advise, but not veto or vote upon contracts to which they are not a party. The Chair should alternate between the parties on the sub-committees.

7. It would be the duty of the whole JCT (or a representative smaller executive grouping of it) to ensure that the documents all interlock fully with each other. It should also supervise the preparation of any other documents necessary to complete the matrix including bonds, warranties, latent defects insurance and special conditions for design undertaken by contractors or specialist subcontractors. Such documents might require ad hoc groupings to formulate them, or could be dealt with by the appropriate sub-committees.

CCSJC

8. The CCSJC currently consists of nine members. There are three each from the Institution of Civil Engineers, the Association of Consulting Engineers and the Federation of Civil Engineering Contractors, representing clients, consultants and main contractors respectively. I recommend that:-

1. Clients should nominate six members. Three should come from the Construction Clients' Forum and three seats should be taken by Government Departments, two for the Department of Transport and the other to be allocated by the DOE.

2. That the ICE and the ACE be both seen as representing consultants, and each have three seats, making six in total.

3. That the CIEC has six seats.

4. That the CLG has six seats.

5. Alternatively, if the ICE wishes to continue to represent clients, it could be in the clients college, in which case the ACE, the CIEC and CLG could have eight seats each.

9. The CCSJC should then divide itself into similar working parties as suggested for the JCT (see paragraphs 5 and 6), for the purposes of preparing a full matrix of documents based on the principles of Chapter 5.18, including consultants' conditions of engagement, main contracts, subcontracts, bonds etc. As the New Engineering Contract already incorporates many of these principles, it would be best if it were used as the basis for the work of the committees.

National Construction Contracts Council

10. The JCT and the CCSJC should create a joint liaison committee to ensure that the two organisations work closely together. They should eventually merge into a National Construction Contracts Council.

Appendix V

Note by the CIC:
An Analysis of Action in Relation to the Recommendations
of the "Crossing Boundaries" Report
(At 15 APRIL 1994)

Recommendations directed towards the professional institutions in construction

a.   *promote multi-disciplinary undergraduate and postgraduate degrees and greater commonality in professional education with particular emphasis on design, technology and basic management skills*

There is clearly a greater desire amongst professional bodies to encourage the recognition of multi-disciplinary degrees and greater commonality. There has been a significant movement towards the broadening of educational formation in certain disciplines. As specific examples, it is worth citing the new educational framework of the CIOB which is founded on a common core and the final year design project for building services engineers which generally involves active collaboration with architecture students.

b.   *liaise with HEIs (perhaps via CIC) to rationalise the duplication, overlap and repetition in entrance and examination requirements, and to reduce the semantic confusion in descriptions of the subjects taught - bearing in mind the value of diversity*

The professional institutions will have their own established relationships with HEIs and we have no doubt that the issue of entrance requirements is a matter that is discussed on an ongoing basis. However, CIC is not aware of any particular initiative that has been developed as a result of this recommendation.

c.   *give increasing support to the work of the CPD in Construction Group in the development of multi-disciplinary programmes, the maintenance of high quality material, the production of career development guidelines, the encouragement of joint regional initiatives, and reciprocal access to CPD activity*

Following its amalgamation with CIC on 1 January 1994 the active participation of professional institutions in the work of the CPD in Construction Group has increased from 12 to 18. In addition, 8 other members of CIC - research bodies, consulting and trade associations - are also now fully involved in the Group's work. Particular emphasis is being given by the Group to the production and maintenance of good CPD information and career development guidance, the encouragement of joint regional initiatives and reciprocal access to CPD.

d.   *promote obligatory Continuing Professional Development by adopting a bye-law or regulation in their Codes of Conduct which requires the maintenance of professional competence*

Substantial progress has been made in the promotion of obligatory CPD in the professional institutions by a variety of means. 14 of the 18 institutions in membership now have an obligatory status for CPD. In the CIOB, ICE and RTPI this is governed by the Rules/Code of Professional Conduct and in the RIBA and RICS it is governed by a Byelaw under the Royal Charter.

e. *identify and co-ordinate opportunities for appropriate cross-disciplinary industrial experience for undergraduate and postgraduate students*

Following discussions with members, CIC is about to launch (in June 1994) a pilot project which will report to the meeting of Council in September 1994. The aim is to seek to identify the viability of a cross-disciplinary training "brokerage" to be operated from CIC from September 1995 onwards. The objective of the initiative is anticipated to be the co-ordination of training placements/industrial experience periods for undergraduate and postgraduate students across the construction disciplines.

f. *agree common criteria for accreditation possibly leading to a single body to oversee the accreditation of all professional courses in the built environment*

There is some evidence of greater co-operation between professional institutions in the accreditation of courses of mutual interest but there is no evidence of any consideration of a single body to oversee the accreditation of all professional courses in the built environment.

g. *promote improvements in the measurement of skill and ability levels in the output of first degree courses prior to the award of Chartered Status with corresponding promotion and co-ordination of cross-skill industrial training opportunities*

With the current "free-market" in education the work of institutions in the accreditation process is increasingly focusing upon standards as opposed to content. In this context, we find that all professional institutions have given much deliberation to the measurement of ability in their own assessment processes prior to the award of Corporate membership, whether of Chartered or Non-chartered status.

h. *encourage the extension of reciprocal membership arrangements and open access to institutional facilities such as bars, restaurants, libraries and learned society activities*

To a certain extent, and at a limited level, reciprocal arrangements have been encouraged through CIC itself as the product of itinerant meetings around the various institutions' headquarters. However, little is known about multi-lateral, general arrangements between members of different institutions.

Recommendations directed to the HEI's

a. *assemble and publish a register of courses involving some degree of commonality and multi-disciplinary education in construction, and keep it up to date*

b. *publicise successful multi-disciplinary relationships between adjacent Universities and ex-Polytechnics in the field of the built environment and encourage new liaisons*

c.   *launch a forum or fora (perhaps on a regional basis), of academics and associated practitioners active in the field of multi-disciplinary education for the exchange of information and experience, the development of new academic techniques and, with the support of the professional institutions, to provide advice on the promotion and monitoring of multi-disciplinary courses and their implications for the host institution*

d.   *encourage and fund the dissemination of information about interdisciplinarity and commonality*

e.   *tackle problems associated with different course lengths and lack of synchronicity*

f.   *review the geographical location and viability of degree courses for the construction professions with a view to a more rational and cost-effective distribution*

CIC has no evidence to suggest that there has been significant progress in any of these areas. In fact the "free market" culture in higher education will now tend to militate against sharing information about course developments which may be seen to give away commercial advantage amongst competitors.

The CIC retains a high regard for the Built Environment Education Services (BEEDS) and its useful newsletter as a means of providing information on commonality. However, it remains very much a mono-University initiative.

As a specific initiative, CIC is closely involved with a consortium of four Universities in the development of a Credit Accumulation and Transfer Scheme (CATS) for the Built Environment. Details of this scheme are now being finalised and we anticipate a public announcement later this year.

Recommendations directed at CIC

a.   *actively support the work of the CITB and others in promoting the construction industry in schools and discuss with Government the need to establish a broader A level base* **for entrants to the industry and to improve their academic skills**

CIC has retained a close association with the CITB and continues to actively support its work in the development of Curriculum Centres throughout the UK.

b.   *act urgently to implement existing proposals for a whole-industry careers service in Schools, making sure that young professionals are directly involved*

Under CIC's auspices, an industry wide group was formed during 1993 to establish the potential for a whole-industry approach to CIC. This group reported to its constituent bodies in June 1993 and a copy of the report is enclosed. As a result of the report, the inaugural meeting of the Construction Careers Forum was held on 28 March 1994. The Forum brings together CIC, CIEC, CITB, the Junior Liaison Organisation, individual firms and other organisations. Although an independent body, it is based at CIC and managed by CIC staff.

c.   *pursue ways of providing career ladders in education and institutions for technicians and incorporated professionals*

d.   *promote commonality between the Non-Chartered Institutions and act as a catalyst to bring related Institutions together*

The CIC Education & Training Committee established a working party to consider these issues under the Chairmanship of Elizabeth Spark (ASI). This group concluded that the "templating" exercise in mapping NVQ units would provide an opportunity for individual institutions to select their common core, following which the true extend of the need for commonality would become apparent.

e.   *seek a solution to the anomaly created by Incorporated Engineers being recognised in the EC First Directive, whereas their counterparts elsewhere in construction are not*

A small working group of members of the Non-Chartered College of CIC has been established to consider this issue.

f.   *give maximum support to the CPD in Construction Group, and encourage an amalgamation with CIC, in order to fully develop its potential*

As discussed earlier, the amalgamation between CIC and the CPD in Construction Group took place on 1 January 1994

g.   *promote the use of non-adversarial contracts and procurement methods*

CIC has viewed the Latham Review as the opportunity for this purpose.

h.   *promote a study of the Staff College concept to provide a basis for further informed discussion*

A brief paper on the Staff College concept has been prepared by CIC. A task force has been established for the purpose of this study under the Chairmanship of Mike Cottell OBE.

i.   *give full support to the integrative role of building services design and the need to raise standards of performance in this field to improve the overall quality of our buildings and their environmental performance*

There is no specific initiative in this area but CIC has ensured that the point is made at every appropriate opportunity.

j.   *seek discussions with the Engineering Council to examine the effect of their plans for the future of the role of construction engineers in the CIC and in Schools or Departments of the Built Environment. We particularly emphasise our concern for the problems of Building Services Engineering in this respect*

No such discussions have been held.

k.   *Promote the case for a minimum four year full-time or equivalent period of part time study for undergraduate degree courses in all skills*

This issue underpins CIC's basic policy in relation to the education of construction professionals.

l.   *make the Government and the HEFCs aware of the financial implications of increasing the degree of commonality in construction education*

m. *make urgent representations to the Government and the HEFCs on the divisive and damaging effects of present funding policies on the development of multi-disciplinary education and the need to establish a rational basis for the funding of different vocational courses*

Appropriate representations have been made, but it is acknowledged that this needs to be continued.

n. *give detailed consideration to the needs of the construction professions in exploiting any multi-disciplinary opportunities which may arise through NVQs and seek to establish a Joint Awarding Body for NVQs at professional levels*

CIC managed a research project in relation to the question of awarding bodies for higher-level NVQs in the built environment.

The research project was completed in April 1994 and has been considered by the Council's Education & Training Committee.

Following these discussions it has been recommended that CIC should establish an NVQ Committee to co-ordinate members' activities and encourage collaboration between them in the development of NVQs at professional levels. If agreed by members, this Committee would develop proposals for CIC to become an awarding body. This proposal will be considered by the Council in June 1994.

o. *press government and CISC to allow more time and provide more funds for the development of NVQs at levels 4 and 5*

p. *urgently seek increased Government funding to develop and market the NVQ programme and extend its time-scale*

These representations have been pursued at every opportunity.

"We have proposed that the actions needed to implement the Latham Report recommendations should be undertaken by a joint industry Government body which we propose should be called "Construction Sourcing".

"Construction Sourcing" should become recognised by large and small clients, including both new and regular customers of the industries, as a centre for reliable independent advice on how to contract for construction, including building, and civil, electrical, mechanical and process engineering. To meet this role, it must be seen to be led by experienced and knowledgeable clients, but it will need the support of all the professions and industries. We propose the following mission statement, objectives and tasks.

Mission Statement

To assist UK construction industries to become, and to be seen as, "internationally competitive".

To improve the quality of UK construction and reduce the average costs by at least 30% within five years, and to introduce total continuous improvement programmes.

Key Tasks

Promote the implementation of the "Latham Project Action Plan".

Encourage the immediate/early implementation of specific recommendations and develop method statements, priorities and programmes for general or "motherhood" recommendations.

Establish "the cohesive voice for industry clients" as proposed by the Rt Hon John Gummer MP and promote the role of clients as the catalyst of change. We see the clients' groups operating at two levels :

- CEOs committed to directing the introduction of "best practice" through client initiatives,

- procurement professionals to propose and implement the initiatives.

Provide a continuing forum for the exchange of ideas between clients and the industries as established by Sir Michael Latham and led by an independent chairman or a major client.

---

[104] *Source: CIPS final report "Productivity and Costs"*

Support the "re-engineering" of the structure and processes of the industries so as to improve their profitability whilst sharing the benefits with clients and sub-contractors throughout the supply chain.

Establish the "National Construction Contracts Council" to produce and develop the recommended single family of conditions of contract. The council should include representatives of industries and the professions but should be led by clients. No single organisation should have the right of veto.

Sponsor research into project and contract management, with particular emphasis on how best to satisfy the clients' requirements. Co-ordinate and promote the results. Ensure that existing research results from UK and world-wide sources are not overlooked.

Develop "empowerment" programmes for the private and public sectors.

Identify "world-class best practices" and develop "best UK contracting practices" for clients, architect/engineers, other professionals, contractors, sub-contractors and suppliers.

Identify methods of establishing what is "best value for money" and how to implement them.

Sponsor "methodology" projects in public and private sectors.

Produce guidelines of best practice (including guidelines on ethical practice throughout the supply chain) taking account of CUP guidelines and other UK/international publications.

Promote best practice by:

- increasing the awareness of clients, particularly at CEO level

- encouraging the development and promotion of Education and Training programmes for the construction supply chain with clients, employers, the professions, universities and training organisations

- improving communications, particularly through IT

- providing an advisory service

- publicising its services.

Introduce a system to measure the success of each initiative

Direction

We **recommend** that, under the guidance of the Minister and his high level team, "Construction Sourcing" should be directed by a small group able to represent the interests of the industry and its clients. Members of this and associated bodies recommended should have significant relevant experience and could be chosen from :

- The Department of the Environment

- Confederation of British Industry

- Construction Industry Council

- Construction Industry Employers Council

- Specialist Engineering Contractors Group

- National Specialist Contractors Council

- Institute of Directors

- British Property Federation

- European Construction Institute/Business Round Table/Major Projects Association

- Chartered Institute of Purchasing and Supply

However, as we expect that clients (including Government clients) will be the prime movers for change, we **recommend** that "Construction Sourcing's" direction should include substantial representation from clients committed to its objectives at chief executive level.

Profile and Location

We **recommend** that "Construction Sourcing" should be located in a high profile but independent organisation and suggest that the CBI or IoD should be invited to host the office."

Printed in the United Kingdom for HMSO
Dd 0298298   C10   9/94   3400   65536   293178   33/30758